Gang Stalking

The Threat to Humanity

Dr. Corkin Cherubini

Dr. P. A. Angelini. Editor

GANG STALKING: THE THREAT TO HUMANITY.
Second Edition
Copyright © 2014 by Dr. Corkin Cherubini.
All rights reserved.
Printed in the United States of America.
ISBN: 13: 978-1500422936

Editor's Note

During the past ten months, a world we would just as soon not know exists has made itself quite evident. The following pages document the discovery of this shadow world and the covert strategies used to taunt, torture, and eventually murder innocent citizens.

After retiring from the school system in which we had worked for over twenty-five years, we were involved in *dozens* of *activist* concerns. We structured our lifestyle around these concerns and held a fairly steady course, even as *forces* of which we were unaware were melting our minds and scorching our bodies with microwave radiation.

At every turn, there was adversity and interference. We had never heard of *Targeted Individuals*. Not a word anywhere. Even though we were activists/whistleblowers, we had never heard of the Secret Holocaust, the *Silent Holocaust*, the Nazi/Stasi FBI derivative of COINTELPRO, or the most *criminal* program the world has ever had: *Gang Stalking.*

Gang Stalkers are not teenage gangs, not drug groups, but a million times worse: they are government subsidized gangs of millions who target Whistleblowers, activists, minorities, writers, single women, elders—and anyone whom a powerful person may want to be put into a torture/murder program.

The result is a war upon innocent American citizens who are *stymied* in their efforts to fight back against the millions. The media will not expose what is going on. Too often, law enforcement balks at investigating reports of chemical dousing or directed energy attacks and refers the victim to EPA or Poison Control or some other agency that refers the victim back to the police. Yet, with "their" unlimited resources and "their" military/covert weaponry: electronic/microwave weapons, chemicals, and remote chip implantation, *"they"* are able to ***totally control*** the individual.

A mere ten months ago, no one could have convinced us that such a program could exist in the U.S.A. Ironically, my husband has been a major target in the Gang Stalking program for eighteen years. We do not want to see one more person suffer the trauma, the indignities, the disease and/or death that results from being targeted. Instead, we want to see the total elimination of agencies that thrive on murder, assassination, mind control, prostitution rings, heroin trafficking complicity, chaos, confusion, death, and destruction. They must be ended. NOW! (With no new similar, by another name, covert programs put in their place.) We want to see privacy, equality, and humanity restored to our society immediately!

—Dr. P. A. Angelini

iv

Dedication

To my wife and family, of course. Without family and friends, this collection may never have surfaced.

To Mr. James Gibson, activist and freedom fighter, the bravest.

To the many thousands of people who wrote, called, and/or visited during the mid 90's. Apologies from this writer for not being able to respond to the mountains of well-wishers.

To all the **Targeted Individuals** I have met or whose stories I have read during the past year and to those **TI's** whose stories have been buried beneath the secrecy of a covert enterprise.

To all of those who have offered assistance to **TI's**, whether law enforcement, local, state, or national legislators, or private citizens. These people have tried to help **TI's** survive the **most atrocious criminality** the world has ever known.

Any and all profits (100%) derived from sales or donations from this book will go to charitable (human and civil rights) organizations.

Contents

Introduction

Starting in early September, 2013, five months of my life were spent in confusion and disarray. The first two weeks I was in a rental car, and I actually thought the police, secret police, and government agencies were mistaking me for some kingpin criminal who had rented the SUV before I got it!

But the plethora of vehicles continued once I had returned my rental. Every large town and small village—municipal, as well as unmarked vehicles, tailing, watching, STALKING.

Several large, and very loud, black military-looking planes skimmed over our trees and house, and the visits and hoverings by huge black, unmarked helicopters continued to be a concern. What really set me on edge was the helicopter that followed me on a country road before skimming over our car roof.

From Alabama to New England, the unusual array of municipal and unmarked vehicles *everywhere* we went strongly indicated *government involvement.* We knew their agencies controlled the internet and cell phones. They were probably monitoring every word, every move we made. We had long suspected we were possibly under surveillance. We suspected microwave torture. Any talk was in the closet or under layers of blankets and foam.

The journal that begins August 30, 2013, shows the confusion, disbelief, and horror that a typical Targeted Individual might experience . . . not knowing what is going on . . . not aware that he/she has been chosen as a target for the most *criminal program to ever exist*—a program combining elements of the sinister FBI COINTELPRO and the absolute horror of CIA's MK ULTRA, Stasi and Nazi elements, high tech elements, and the basest use of psychology imaginable.

In my case (and probably in most others), *days* and *months* were *spent searching for reasons, well intentioned reasons* that might be linked to *surveillance and stalking.* What had I done to arouse Homeland Security or NSA suspicions? Had I said things about the CIA that could have invoked ire? Had they sorted through thousands of conversations, sarcastic, jocular phrases, momentary creative fictional items, and pillow talk?

Yes, "they" can make something out of *anything*. But all my reasoning came back to the *Whistleblowing* events of the mid-90's. Always.

The only existence I could imagine that seemed similar was that of war refugees. I thought of Anne Frank and family. Often.

I decided to record events for one hundred days—if we lasted that long. Again, we did not know of anything in our society that compared to our situation. Not that we are generally uninformed or naïve. I would usually read many hours of alternative news sites each week. Many **different** news sites such as Alternet, Counterpunch, and Adbusters. But we had never heard of anything similar to what we were experiencing in either the big or small media.

In February of 2014, I was hit four times in one day with what was some form of direct energy weapon (DEW). The fourth was incapacitating for at least a half an hour. My vision was destroyed for an hour, and my heart seemed to be having great difficulty.

As much as I did not want "them" to know what we were reading, I went online. Typing in the symptoms brought up an entire *world* I had never heard mention of:

the world of *Targeted Individuals*. A world of *Gang Stalking* victims or *Organized* or *Group Stalking* victims.

Some relief flooded over us: at least we knew what the torturous, murderous program was, and we knew others were in the same boat. Whistleblowers to working, single moms. Writers to dissidents. Millions. I read the stories of agonizing torture and saw long lists of Targeted Individuals who had died young from cancers induced by microwave radiation. I read of the many who were so tortured they committed suicide. I read of those who were sick and dying from the poisons and drugs covertly pumped into their homes and cars. I looked at my wife and myself—both on a fast track to death after decades of microwaving. And, of course, the usual poisons and drugs flooding all our environs with covert precision. No one would ever be charged for these murders.

I agonized day and night for us, but especially for those much younger—some with children, for the children would be destroyed along with their parents, just as the family pets would be.

I blew a shrill whistle once, in the 90's, and I knew I would be the Whistleblower once more. Older, likely dying from the effects of radiation and poisons, but with a resolve to persist until the whistle is sounding in every American's ears, alerting each and every one about the **MOST ATROCIOUS CRIMINAL PROGRAM THE WORLD HAS EVER KNOWN!**

August 30, 2013

Freedom. *Liberty.* *Equality.* *Justice.* Words like these had a special meaning to me for over half a century. But today, those words no longer signify what was once cherished American ideals.

Truth, which has often been difficult to pin down, has become ever more ethereal; after all, six corporate conglomerates control what information we ingest.

One recent phenomenon that the world seems to finally be waking up to is the total invasion of individual privacy—so total that the word, *TOTAL*, has taken on a new connotation.

Each and every phone conversation is not just tapped into, but recorded and stored on massive hard drives. Ditto for email and internet browsing habits. In fact, most every transaction and move we make finds its way into somebody's data banks readily available for data mining. Already more than a little scary, but there are even worse things occurring, so much worse that a book, which began as a mostly humorous collection has turned sadly realistic, presenting what many are promoting as the "new norm."

September 1, 2013

My wife and I drove over the knoll on a country lane that led to our very *private* home. Private no more. Over the house was a large black helicopter (the kind we thought were just in fictional movies). It hovered there, looking as if it might be ready to land on the roof!

The huge machine remained there until we turned into the long tree-lined drive. We pulled into the carport and sat, speechless for a few moments. Then, we hazarded a few guesses as to what the machine was doing there: looking for a lost child or a criminal or a marijuana farm or . . . . Nothing made sense. It was hovering just over our roof!

In a couple of days, we forgot to worry about it or even to think about it. Much odder things had happened, we thought.

Many weeks later, I was working in the yard when what had to be an identical helicopter roared slowly over the house. It circled and clattered over again. Then, it circled the three acre lot <u>several</u> times!

I choked, quit working, and went inside. Had we done something and didn't know it? Was this just some perverted form of terrorism by air? Intimidation?

The house sat, invisible and "private" behind hedges and thick tree growth in the rural boondocks, ten miles from Alabama, twenty-five from Georgia, and about sixty-five from Mississippi. Maybe we needed to research what "drive by" and hovering copters might be doing. (An ironic note here is for a few years we had lived just four and a half air miles from one of the largest helicopter training schools in the world, yet we *never* experienced anything like the hovering buzzing that we were being subjected to now.) Should we call the local police? In the past, our experience with them had been positive. Still, large black helicopters didn't seem like anything the local police would be involved with. We would wait. We had been to a few peace rallies and anti-nuclear meetings. Probably, we were on somebody's list, just like all the real activists. And many *non*-activists.

Then, sliding into bed, a few days or maybe a week or so after the slow, multi-circling copter, we noticed the spots, quarter and half dollar sized pink and red circles that became brighter and darker red and grew in size during the next few weeks. The spots bothered us because we are, and have been for thirty years, organic food and super clean water health advocates. So healthy, I don't have a physician.

Quick initial research took us to the internet. One of the first pages we looked at was about the Fukushima children's problems. Top of the early problem list: *eczema*.

We'd heard of it, but went to another site for pictures. It was as if someone had taken photos of our arms and legs. The Fukushima children tended to be confused and dizzy, just as we had been the past few weeks. Forgone was our rigorous exercise, jogging with our two dogs, and even our at-home yoga. As the days passed, we grew sicker and dizzier. Could we conceivably be getting nuked by a big black helicopter?

Research took us to a 2004 book called <u>Homeland Security</u>, edited by Norris Smith and Lynn Messina. We learned that inspectors use cesium to produce a powerful gamma ray to scan the contents of steel-walled containers arriving at the ports of Los Angeles and Long Beach, CA.

Cesium?   Gamma rays?   Other ports use x-rays. Could such technology be used to scan the homes of private citizens? If so, who would be authorized to do the scanning and for what purpose, if indeed there were any authorization or *legitimate* purpose?   And how would such scanning be accomplished? By helicopter? The information we had unearthed was devastating in its possible implications.

"We've been ravaged," my wife whispered hoarsely.

"Sounds like a death warrant from . . . ?"

"It's not just the health hazard. We've had intruders who know where every item we own is located!"

Did I sense near hysteria in her voice? "There's no reason!"

"They'll find one. But they're probably responsible to no one."

"Remember reading that *any* exposure is bad? We don't even like the dentist making x-rays. But these spots are the result of something far more intense than an occasional dental x-ray. Makes the night stalker, if there really was one, seem like a saint."

"No! No! No! No!"

"And to think our tax dollars may be supporting such tactics!"

We talked for hours. Mostly one line exclamations. Sleep was out of the question.

We were only teachers. Thousands of students had passed through our classes. We knew English and education for thirty years, and now we were in retirement, both about seventy.

We stood and watched as the big, black helicopters kept circling around us. Why? Why? What is happening?

If we had had any knowledge that the big black helicopters held the power of death over us—just as the German Gestapo Nazis ushered Jews into the gas ovens, we might have tried running and running and running and running—running till our hearts stopped. But you can't run from a helicopter or its death rays; you remain paralyzed.

"Microwave mind control is the biggest threat to humanity and the most sinister plan to enslave the human race forever.
--Dr. Rauni Leena Kilde
From "Microwave Mind Control"

September 5, 2013

4:00 A. M.

One mostly horrible week has passed since I last wrote, but a journal—a diary of sorts—recording events and observations might be worthwhile.

For me, sleep was difficult for several nights. I possibly averaged about three hours per night.

Looking back at my pocket calendar, I'll note that five days ago we cleared the floor of a small, centrally located closet as a hiding spot if the helicopter came again. A top shelf we loaded with books and clothing. Yes, it was probably a waste of time for one primary reason: absurdly inadequate. But you try to do something.

My mother turned 93 several days ago. She has been in "therapy" for a number of weeks after almost a week in the hospital. We go by most every day, and she can tell something is amiss, but we don't mention details.

Also, I went by the sheriff's office to see if they might know why a helicopter would be hovering around. The representative I talked with knew nothing about the activities. He said that usually such maneuvers were just checking for marijuana farms.

I told him that was my first thought, but the house-hovering and flight frequency (five or six times that we knew about) made us wonder. I mentioned that I'd heard that guns might be a possible cause, and I did have several that were mostly antique inherited items, the largest rifle being a .22. I added that any visit with detection devices was fine with me. I would be happy to cooperate. He smiled and said it was probably nothing to worry about.

I felt better after the visit. Much better. I went home and took a one hour nap, and that night, I slept well. Doubts and worries began to creep back the next day, however. My wife does much better. I recall reading somewhere that men are the real worriers. A generalization, but I was feeling certain, again, that stress could take a few years off of one's life expectancy. If there was much expectancy left after the hovering copters.

September 6, 2013

I have the same symptoms that I kept for four years in the deep, rural south when I was school superintendent dealing with long-standing civil rights violations. The shallow breathing—short quick breaths. Extreme loss of sleep—averaging three to four hours per night at best. Nervous energy going nowhere. And mental activity that was, at times, almost like several powerful computers spitting out both relevant and tangential information without regard for coherence.

I could not stop thinking of one particular phone call from an African American school administrator who said she had been through a nightmare situation similar to mine. But hers crumpled quickly--due to the extreme stress. She told me I would have health problems, too.

They would be mental *and* physical. She said she believed health deterioration was unavoidable, to please take care. I answered that I was sorry, yet proud for what she had tried to accomplish. I added that I might escape the severe problems because I did vigorous exercise in fifteen to twenty minute bursts several times a day.

She paused, then told me that she didn't believe a person could avoid it. The health would be compromised. She said again, "Please be careful." Another pause. "You know, they shot down three of our greatest leaders. *They* can get anybody."

I told her not to worry, that I thought about those tragedies every single day. And I still do. And about the *they*, now that more evidence has come to light in books, articles, and documentary film clips on YOU TUBE. The *They* are still with us, more in control than ever.

As for the health, I think she was right. If *they* don't get you one way, there are many, many more ways.

In a way, I want to keep writing and writing—entire chapters per day. In another way, I would prefer that entries be more like my exercise and breathing—short bursts and breaths. But hopefully, not too shallow.

September 8, 2013

Sunday.

Yesterday, an anti-nuclear power (or at least "safer" nuclear power) group hosted a small conference at a nearby—fifteen minutes away—conference center. A couple of years ago, after the Fukushima meltdown, they had met with a Japanese TV film crew present. We went, and I ended up doing an interview for Japanese TV (supposedly). I never found out for certain. The interview concerned what I thought the implications of the current meltdown might be for nuclear power. I certainly did not want to make waves or bring attention to myself, but I still wonder if the local power company might have been displeased with what I said.

The meeting: about twenty attendees, almost all well over fifty-five. Where were the thirty year old moms and the college crowd? Quite possibly the meeting could not have accommodated many more. Most of it ended up being a work/planning meeting. The climax of the day was when the group voted to buy a roughly twenty thousand dollar state of the art radiation detector/monitor. A commendable move since many people have trouble believing "nuclear event news" from the nuclear industry—or the various governments!

I quietly asked a few familiar faces if they knew about any dangers associated with helicopter surveillance—and specifically, super powerful x-rays.

Zero! No one had heard of any helicopter use except for marijuana farm searches. Ultimately, this group seemed to know about monitoring radiation levels and general dangers of nuclear, and that is positive. I was surprised that x-ray surveillance was not part of their knowledge base. But then, neither is it part of my own, and I read a lot!

What is so disappointing to me is that we humans are relegated to such a minute area of expertise, often having little hope of getting the bigger and clearer picture. With technological complexity burying us, we are like the auto factory worker, who does okay mounting his particular wheel bolt eight hours a day, but has no inkling of the thousands of intricacies that it took to create the car. The individual is totally subservient to those with extensive manpower, money, and means—the big corporations or the government. I fear them both.

I plan to refrain from any further internet research, most any phone calls, and even checking out of library materials, including duplication, until I can meet with a knowledgeable attorney and try to get a grasp on what is happening.

September 15, 2013

Sunday.

One week later. I am now in New England, about 1,500 miles north of southern Tennessee. Combined business and pleasure trip. Except my mind is overactive concerning the big black copters. I think about the twelve college age kids I saw at a meeting who spoke about their part in a Chicago World Bank protest. The copters were prolific and ever present. Vietnam again. What worked okay on the battlefields will work even better on our own citizens.

Over a thousand miles and way over a million thoughts.

I stopped in Portland, ME, and dropped by the ACLU office, without an appointment. (No phones or internet if there is any other way!) My stop was almost useless, except the guy on duty did confirm what I had assumed—that any legal investigation must be done in the state of occurrence.

The state of injustice in America is common knowledge to many Americans, but for minorities anywhere, it seems especially unbalanced. A power structure with all the audacity and arrogance and raw power of a president starting a war for *no good reason*. (My thoughts are whirling much faster than my pen, and the smooth, coherent flow of a polished writer may be absent. Still, this writing is just an attempt to journalize—in a sort of streaming consciousness—my feelings and observations.)

State of occurrence and state of injustice. The point being that my own background (outsider and, especially, one trying to champion civil rights) may not have been an asset in rural southern America.

I clearly recall, as if it were yesterday, when a small town power structure went public against me personally. From that moment, there was hardly a person who was not fearful of being in my presence. Twenty years of collegial friendship vanished in a moment. And I hardly blamed them. In fact, I always encouraged the distance. The last thing I wanted was for anyone to suffer at the hands of this power structure on my account.

Again and again, the *solidarity of evil* came to my mind. Back to a tenth grade math class in the south, my first full year there. The teacher stopped talking and went to the window and watched. Soon a few others went to the windows. Then, we were all at the windows.

The U-shaped building allowed us to see another entire wing; they were all at the windows too. The object of silent, unanimous concern was one black child walking up the school drive. As he got close to the front door, we lost sight for a few seconds. Then, he was leaving.

Quickly. Half way down the drive, he began running. Soon, word came that he was only delivering a note from the black school.

The talk of the day was what would happen if they ever tried to integrate.

I spent half a year in junior high and a full tenth grade year in the south. Then, four years of college. And, much like everyone I knew from the south (*or* the north), I developed some prejudices, too. Most were readily dealt with, but there have been those moments I've had to wonder about. But I think people of every race have had racist or sexist or prejudiced moments.

September 18, 2013

Wednesday

Visits to Orono and Belfast libraries in the last two days yield very little information of the type I need. A librarian in Belfast said to go on internet for technical things. Suggested using their library computers when I mentioned I was being well-tracked. She said that everyone seems nervous now—including herself. Again, it seems heinous that people should be so paranoid of their own government's intentions.

My first cup of coffee thoughts were apropos this morning:

(1) **Why** every single person alive should fear this spying military-police state; and

(2) **What** "small" moves we can bravely take to start a return to normalcy.

First, why we should **all** fear. I have always thought that the wealthy and famous "high profilers" had a huge advantage over the little guy in a two room cabin off the grid. Indeed, this little guy could have a fatal accident, or just disappear, and hardly an eyebrow would be raised. But recent events in my own life—and home—have me thinking that the high profilers might often be on thin ice, as well.

It could be the home of the little guy in the cabin or a high ranking official or a wealthy "liberal" who might have made waves. It could be **anyone**. No **real** reason needed (but they would certainly have one ready anyway).

Of course, they probably won't find anything at all, much less anything that is meaningful or concrete. But, they have their pictures. Plenty and plenty of pictures. X-ray pictures. Very, very powerful x-rays. X-rays that can easily pierce through homes, businesses, or multi-level apartments. They have pictures of your jewelry. They have pictures of your coin collection. Maybe a priceless painting, violin, guitar, antique. BUT, more importantly, they have X-RAY PICTURES OF YOU! Not medical x-rays, but x-rays with the power to pierce through heavy layers of steel and/or concrete. Yes, they have their "routine check" pictures of everything you own, and your and your wife's and your children's

> *"The new controllers of the world will be the ones who are stockpiling trillions of terabytes of surveillance records. They will produce only the data they want to make public; they will suppress all else. They will control the past history and the future as well."*
> —*Dr. Corkin Cherubini*

pictures in x-ray vision.

I have not used the internet to see just *how* dangerous and deadly the x-ray program might be, but at this point, it certainly doesn't take *any* imagination to fear the worst. For everyone.

For decades, I have read of the dangers of well-controlled medical x-rays, especially mammograms and head/brain scans. One doctor's site stated that x-rays cause more cancer than all other things combined! I would have guessed chemicals to be more dangerous, but he had substantial basis for his claim. Again, these were medical x-rays, possibly not even in the same realm as the spy helicopter x-rays that have the power to pierce roofs, floor levels, and metal containers.

So, they stop using x-rays. What else do they have? An untold array of some of the most deadly germs (bio) and chemicals that the brains of devious people in the world could come up with. Most of these weapons can be found on a couple of U. S. military bases.

But back to the essence of this page. A system that has the power (both surveillance power and killing power) that our military has is dangerous to every person alive. And with fifty odd thousand swat teams sitting around, and all the armaments and personnel that monstrously huge Homeland Security budgets can buy, when they can no longer find much of anyone to blame for anything, they can and will start going for anyone who might squeak a word of dissent.

Tonight, in Belfast, ME, there is an award winning documentary about the "**War on Whistleblowers**." The question the announcement poster featured was, "Who's next?" All I could think was, "I can't believe it's me!"

I have given NSA many thousands of words of dissent, often trying to explain to my own mother that her FOX news is not giving her the whole picture. I make certain she hears (she's very hard of hearing) the side that I read on many alternative news sites, and I try to read many because I know any one site often has its own agenda. Also, different news sites tend to specialize in certain types of content. Some excel in providing insights into a sick economy, while others delve deeper in foreign policy, militarism, loss of freedom, or contamination of our planet. Most people I've met think they can "feel their way through the fluff" to get to the truth much of the time. Perhaps . . .

Yesterday, I had a long conversation with a well-read Vietnam era veteran. I told him that on several recent occasions I had awakened at about two or three a.m. in sort of a mental paralysis, just from thinking about the monstrous forces I am/was up against. His contention was that their perceived stranglehold is not as great as it seems. Much of the fear that paralyzes us is psy-ops. At first, I was happy to agree, and I felt some relief. But relief was brief. I can surmise the power of unlimited resources.

This morning, before dawn, I thought about my life as a whistleblower in the mid-90's. I survived, barely. Barely—with some luck, a lot of work, and scores of sleepless nights. That was in 1994, 1995, and 1996, trying to survive against a power structure in one small county. Just a few dozen were really driving for my destruction, but a few hundred were following nicely.

From 1996 to 2013, the country has changed. A different type of media, I hear and feel. Then, the "Patriot" Act. The stamped in stone guarantee that our liberty has ended. The "Patriot" Act has NSA (and CIA, *et. al*) as all watching, worse than Orwellian, surveillance tools. If Orwell and Bradbury could return and see how far we have regressed beyond their own dystopian vision, I would expect them to stare in disbelief and utter: "THIS IS THE SOCIETY THAT

EVEN HITLER COULD NOT HAVE CONCEIVED!"

I recently asked someone what they thought the next level of surveillance might be. Depressingly, the response was precisely the answer that I had—the one that inspired asking the question: RFID chips. Under the skin. Monitoring every move. Every word. Possibly prompting us just how to behave. Rewarding us with a sensory pleasure flow if we obey. And punishing "wayward" acts.

This technology is already here. Now! Waiting to be fully implemented. And improved upon. Yearly upgrades for our chips. And, like our cell phone tracking devices, they will help someone find you if you have Alzheimer's and wander away. An extremely poor excuse to chip everyone unless the person in question has advanced dementia and a history of wandering. Even then . . .

Yet, before the chips, they still have us with their laser surveillance, satellite surveillance, drone surveillance. The list seems never-ending! Many of us will not accept this gross invasion of privacy. But we are a dying generation. Already, they are preparing our children and grandchildren. Hitler was not worried, either, about the dissidents who would not accept the Nazi doctrine, saying confidently, *"I have your children."*

September 20, 2013

Friday.

I went back to Belfast for the documentary movie/meeting on Wednesday. Arrived early and casually alluded to my situation. One elderly person was quick to say I was "probably paranoid—as most *everyone* is these days." All of the people there who were active "knew they were on the list." The same words I'd heard 1,500 miles south! Is it not sad that *any* law abiding American citizen should be on some agency's "list"? I've read that the "lists" include many, many millions of Americans who are labeled and profiled for something as positive and humane as attending a pro-peace meeting! Or, being a member of any of a hundred or a thousand various peaceful groups.

My huge, overriding concern is: how many of these millions are going to be secretly NUKED or POISONED? Would any of them KNOW?! Much less be able to *prove* any such action against them! Just look back at the effects of agent orange or depleted uranium. A tragic abuse of chemical and nuclear agents that were detrimental to our own people as well as to others. Inhuman, indeed, yet our own government forces denied, with extreme resistance, any responsibility for the residual effects these agents *may* have caused.

Is even one American citizen, no matter how powerful and wealthy, really safe from a furtive onslaught of nuclear and chemical agents. I don't think so. And again, I wonder if the high profile types are just as vulnerable as the average Joe Citizen, but more noticeable. I have a host of questions in my mind that I have wanted to research on the internet. But I even regret having checked out several library books since I don't know how far reaching their methods might be. But the questions are there—waiting. How many might have already died from a mysterious brain or lung or breast cancer? Or the indiscernible illness? Or the "accidents"?

> **"The CIA and the military are carrying out an illegal 'targeted killing' program in which people . . . are . . . killed without charge or trial."**
> —**American Civil Liberties Union**
> **From "Targeted Killings"**

How far can a helicopter project a deadly nuclear beam? Will the millions of small, ubiquitous drones replace the helicopter as the preferred killing system? Will people like me, who think such atrocities could *never* happen to them, ever wake up? And, even if we awaken, what can we do about such heinous force?

Paranoia? Of course. But not without reason. Everyone seems to know a little paranoia is good, but too much can debilitate. Government operatives know this. Just watching and/or "learning" can debilitate or cause irrational behavior.

And, yes, there are those moments of helplessness. If the helicopters are being sent by an arm of our military forces (and I feel more certain of this each day), then I am alive and squirming only because they are allowing it. They have the supreme killing power on the face of this earth, and they also have high tech spy and surveillance systems that defy imagination. They have *total* media control. And they have the sheer power to control every single person and institution in our country and most of the world. Locked into their sights, one might have reason for more than a little paranoia.

It shouldn't be this way, but it is.

Same Day. Evening.

Common Ground Organic Growers Fair was both delightful and informative. The bad part was the drive—almost two hours.

With three social activism tents, there were many to talk with about the state of society. Drones kept coming up as sort of a symbol of what world society would be up against forever and ever.

What made the trip worthwhile was my conversation with an activist about my own age. I made casual mention of the helicopter passes and the ensuing skin maladies, and he instantly said it was probably "hop waves."

I said, "Hop waves? I'm not sure what that is."

"Hop waves are microwaves. They can induce extreme paranoia that can lead to violence and more. Hop. H-A-A-R-P," he spelled out.

"Oh, HAARP! I know a bit about that, but I didn't know about the paranoia," I said, realizing that "hop waves" is how it would be pronounced at this latitude.

"The HAARP signature has been found on many, if not *most,* of the irrational violence perpetrators—like that fellow in Washington. You heard about that last week?"

I said I hadn't heard.

"Well, all indicators seem to point to it being HAARP induced violence. They zero you in, and the force on your brain can have you doing anything."

I mentioned that I'd heard about it as a deliberate cause of earthquakes, but not as a weapon to use directly on individuals' minds. But then, if a billion watts of microwave energy can trigger an earthquake, it does seem quite obvious that it could rearrange gray matter.

"But what about x-rays? How powerful can they get?" I pressed.

"Over a decade ago, a pilot told me that he could see every move a family made—through the house roof—even though he was a mile high in the sky. Over ten years ago."

Others came to the table. I thanked him and walked away.

HAARP! That could explain a lot: the paranoia, the irritability, outbursts, a few racial and sexist slurs, foul language—all since about year 2000. Almost nothing remotely similar before then. Now common.

But why would they be using weapons like HAARP and/or x-rays to debilitate and destroy? On me or others? WHY?

"The first week I knew I was being targeted, I thought, 'They must be spending thousands of dollars for all this municipal vehicle movement!' A few weeks later, I revised that figure to tens of thousands. Now, after reading about how extensive the covert harassment is, the figure is again revised to hundreds of thousands of dollars! No! Millions!"

—Dr. "C"

September 23, 2013

Monday.

Reunited, after a long travel day, with my wife. The travel was more stressful than in times past because of the unusual police presence. The tendency is to want to think they just have to grab a bite or buy something at the truck stop, or stop at the rest stop at the same time you do. But the police presence on my drive home was so totally different from my fifty-five years of prior driving experience. Oh, my dog was with me, and I felt bad that she was cooped up for almost twenty hours. I did give her a few short running breaks, however.

My wife keeps extensive files on everything she sees as really noteworthy, and I remembered her being horrified by the HAARP powers, along with many other scary things. I asked her to pull out anything she had on HAARP, and she wisely said to wait until morning. We are whispering in each other's ears about HAARP, and anything else that might be provocative now. Music plays in the background. I used to read spy novels, never thinking I might end up in one. But the technology in the 80's was only paving the way for what we have today—technology many times more sophisticated.

This morning I began reading notes she had taken on HAARP. I felt palpitations in my chest as I read.

September 24, 2013

Tuesday.

Rather than formal and proper quoting and documenting (I feel a time urgency!), I will loosely paraphrase the notes as I remember from yesterday's reading.

HAARP stands for High Frequency Active Auroral Research Program. Its equipment produces very powerful microwaves that can be beamed to pinpointed locations, for destruction, surveillance, and more. One note said that chemtrails can spread the microwaves. Another note said that vans could carry HAARP equipment (thus helicopters).

Psychiatric problems can be induced by these waves. Jesse Ventura, according to Wikipedia, was concerned about their power to control minds. The UN wanted to ban mind control weapons, but the U.S. said no.

> **"Knowledge is our only defense against mind control."**
> —Dr. "C"

September 25, 2013

Wednesday.

Reading further over notes, I found one section especially horrifying: anyone who is against the establishment or is a whistle blower may be harassed covertly! Legally! And, a Defense Department Directive, 5240 1-R, 1994, states that those under surveillance could be used for *remote experimentation!!*

I thought of the huge dark blood red splotches on both legs, and lay awake from 2:00 A.M. till dawn.

Is my anxiety being caused by HAARP waves, or simply the knowledge that "they" are the world's greatest power and that the power of those involved appears to be totally out of control?

My wife and I are two rather old (70) former academic types, and we are suddenly pitched into battle with the world's most expert assault groups. Thousands, or likely millions, of experts in every area including military, police, covert operatives.

Yes, I am stressed, now. For the good reason just mentioned, and for many other good reasons, probably including HAARP waves and x-rays. (I walked out of my New England cabin just five days ago, about 5:30 P.M., and the sunset brightly illumined a monstrous chemtrail with its fluffy billows on either side of the cabin. Only yesterday did I read that chemtrails are used to spread HAARP waves. I will research the internet again for HAARP, if and when a search becomes less risky. That day may not arrive.)

It is evening. I had to wait too long to start the writing, and I am so tired from lack of rest. Tomorrow

We go to Nashville to try to find advice. This will be my third attempt. Though we will be careful to be unobserved (we don't wish to create even more reaction), I feel as if scores of satellite and building monitors will alert *whoever* has all the sheer power in the world.

October 1, 2013

Tuesday

About a month now since having made the copter/eczema connection. A month of watching your life's dream disintegrate before your eyes and seeing all become ashes in a hell.

I have thought of many tragic/ironic events that may compare, at least a little, to what we are experiencing. There is a couple I know of who finally bought the new super Harley they had wanted for years. On the first ride out, just several blocks from their home, they were struck by a car. They survived, but not without devastating injury. I think about that accident frequently, reminding myself that my situation could be worse.

Still, as one who has hardly ever had a health issue (likely from plenty of exercise and eating a low fat organic whole grain vegan type diet), I am wondering about what the eczema could be a precursor to. The most worrisome problem is lower stomach pain. At times it becomes excruciating—so painful I have to stifle the scream that wants to escape. There was absolutely no sign of such pain until a few months after the helicopters began flying over. (Of course, there may be no connection.)

But physically, that is it. Except for a mild sore throat I've had for just over a month. I've had a few before in my life, but they usually disappear after a few days.

The mental stress is, for the time, as much or more painful than the physical. In the deep south as a superintendent of schools trying to make a few inroads into civil rights abuses, the situation was insanely bad. I won't try to describe it here. It would take dozens of pages to scratch the surface of portraying that horror.

Even at that, the horror was localized. The worst of it was within the borders of one or two smaller counties. A truly investigative media was looking into every aspect of the situation and revealing some things that even I hadn't realized.

> "Trillions are spent on black projects in this country and even Congress doesn't know what it's spent on; well, we now know some of it's being used to attack us."
> —John Mecca
> From "U. S. Government Stalking"

That was the mid-90's. Within less than two decades, our new media seems to many of us to be something a lot more like what we heard about the Russian Pravda, during the worst Communist regime years, not telling the real story at all. A propaganda device only. Possibly, they are under guns, too. But it is discouraging to realize that we cannot depend on our media as we should be able to.

There was tremendous support (calls, letters, visits) from all over the country, but outside the county. Within the county, the African American community was largely supportive. More supportive than seemed humanly possible when we consider the oppression and intimidation they might suffer at every turn.

Now, we seem to have no one. It seems a totally different (hopeless) world. We don't even know who our oppressors are, except that they have large helicopters and some sophisticated weaponry aboard, and that they seem to command all the local and state police in America.

In the 90's I could expect the police tail for a few miles now and then. But it was only there in that county. Now, it is nationwide. The trip to New England was sickening. For miles, they were behind, in front, and on the sides of the road. In areas that a year earlier I could go for weeks and hardly see a patrol car. You think, why should it matter if you're not doing anything wrong? But it does matter. For one thing, you know that if they did decide to step up the harassment, they could find something. Or worse yet, create something. Just doing their jobs with instructions from above. Our own law enforcement seems controlled by the agencies that many of us fear most.

The media difference I mentioned above: I'm not sure even one major media group would be interested in investigating what is going on. Or maybe they don't want their lives devastated.

Another huge difference is that whoever is targeting us has total access to over ten years (possibly twenty) of my private thoughts and phone exclamations. Taken out of context, such words are often used to discredit earmarked individuals.

Also, much of our conversation was tailored for a possible spying audience. There were numerous times that we "acted in a theatre of the absurd" to—sometimes challenge, sometimes show we were part of the deep south environment. We tried many different strategies, but never heard anything.

Nor did things change any. Until I mentioned a law suit.

We feel very strongly that spies, stalkers, and other covert types don't deserve the truth. And even with "truth," they will pick and twist whatever serves their purpose. It was going on in Hamlet's court (Polonius, Claudius, Rosencrantz and Guildenstern), certainly. But it has become infinitely worse than a guy hiding behind your bedroom curtain. Paraphrasing Paul Baird, the electronic surveillance is so enshrouding that it can make us all the equivalent of an electronic POW.

A difference—greater than I want to admit—is that we are now seventy instead of fifty. There just isn't much energy left to deal with the millions of young guys in their various agencies who have unlimited power, money, resources, and a "Patriot" Act to back them to the hilt.

Twenty years ago, I didn't mind a challenge if I thought I had a minute chance to keep my head above water. In this situation, my feeling is less than hopeless. I am not writing this to save myself (I think I was likely atomically murdered as much as a year ago). I just hope something herein will help others.

(Knowledgeable, sharp attorneys? We never found one in Nashville. We went by two offices, but something didn't seem right. Of course, we are "dropping in," not phoning, as I mentioned. I can't blame anyone for not wanting to get involved. It's like David going up against a million giants . . . giants commanding nuclear and state of the art global surveillance.)

October 4, 2013

At 4:00 a.m., I was wondering if the IRS had helicopters. Were they responsible for x-raying our home to determine what we had and where it was located? I had certainly heard the horror stories of how they had targeted people, and this was quite recently. We even talked to two attorneys and one certified accountant about the situation, and they advised us not to worry. Frightening to think workers at such an agency can be ordered to hassle people simply because of their beliefs, not because of any wrong doing.

My next thoughts were about my ninety-three year old mom. She lives in the small town where our river house is located. When we moved her there six years ago, I felt good about the location and her neighbors. An elderly lady lived in the house next door, and they became friends. Mom had her dog and a helper who came several times a week. I was pleased that she could continue to remain independent, something very important to her.

Then, four years ago, the elderly woman next door suddenly moved a few blocks away. My mom never did find out why she had moved. The house has been vacant ever since then, which had all of us puzzled. The most puzzling aspect is that my mom saw two men moving something into the house shortly after her neighbor had moved. At first, she thought she was going to have new neighbors. But no one moved in. Instead, she sees these two men going into the house for a short time at regular intervals—weekly, it seems, and usually at dusk. Another odd thing, a bedroom window in the other house that faces her kitchen and living room, remains open in all kinds of weather. For several years, I ignored her observations and explained to her that it was none of her business what the neighbors were doing. That was before August 30, 2013.

Any odd occurrence summons scores of red flags. As implausible as it may seem, I can't help but wonder if the house is being used as a surveillance point, or possibly something even worse. Such tactics are typical of these stalkers, and family members are often accosted as well as the primary target.

My mom has had several falls during the past six years, and most of them involved stooping over and losing balance. One of the worst, however, was when she stepped into her carport—which faces the empty house—and fell for *no apparent reason*, according to both her and her helper who happened to be a few feet away at the time.

Today is the first time I have thought about that oddity, and the first time it occurred to me that the house next door was conceivably being used for covert purposes. Mom seemed to know from the first that something was not right about the situation. She just didn't know *what*. Still . . .

October 9, 2013

Wednesday.

This entire scenario keeps pointing to what occurred seventeen years earlier: civil rights work. Whistleblower. Major features in major papers and magazines. TV interviews. Likely one of the most noted educational leaders of the century for shining a spotlight on the unfairness and inequity in American schools, from kindergarten on, that the majority of African Americans and other minorities must endure. This is all about ending the life of a whistleblower and activist and the life of his wife. We are one.

I am still not using the internet, as "they" could see the very direction in which my thoughts are moving, and possibly take quick, drastic steps. I do have, however, a forty page printout from a Paul Baird article. My wife was researching weather control (and HAARP) about a year ago for her writing, and came across this piece entitled: "The Truth About Secret Weapons and the Involuntary Testing of Those Weapons on Civilians." That was the title of the internet article, but it may have come from a book or article by Paul Baird entitled "Satellite Tyranny." A longish quote from Baird:

"The U. S. Patriot Act, for example, protects governments and connected criminals from criticism and/or detection and prosecution. Under this act anyone whistleblowing or fighting the system on a major concern is arbitrarily deemed to be unpatriotic."

And:

"They can be listed (by a senior politician or at the request, through them, or a connected criminal) as a security risk and harassed covertly, using secret technologies."

And, same paragraph:

"The victims are not openly confronted as that would remove any feigned excuses and leave the perpetrators open to all manner of accusation. Instead, the methods used are covert; employing high tech to remotely torment and deceive victims without leaving evidence."

The quotes from Baird come horrifyingly close to my own recent experiences. My wife and I are *one*. "They" are many *millions* with totally unlimited resources.

Resources like media, money, political power, unbelievable surveillance powers, manpower in the millions. One person stands no chance whatsoever. I know that. And still I keep writing. To myself, most likely. It's all I have to do.

Civil rights workers of the 50's and 60's knew of these dangers as did some of the antiwar activists. But then, we knew we had a

> "I keep thinking of the rat experiments of the 50's and 60's, and how the lack of privacy and space killed almost every mouse in the experiment. And it was irreversible."
> —Dr. "C"

Constitution to rely on—maybe. Now we have a Patriot Act and x-ray copters and spy and bomb drones.

When I first connected the huge light and dark red eczema with the hovering copters, I knew our lives were already compromised. Some splotches looked as if a giant lamprey had been at work for a few days. An extreme sore throat is always present—so bad it often makes sleep impossible. But the worst health issue is the stomach pains that began shortly after the copters started their hovering.

The total psychological damage "bundle" is enough to overwhelm. We have come to assume that every whisper is being parabolically miked or that remote cameras are recording every move. Sex, and even showering and using the bathroom all feel uncomfortable. Sex, in fact, has stopped almost entirely since the day I began this diary.

Each time I write an entry herein, I wonder if it is all being filmed and read by a spy device or if it is being captured by long-range x-ray cameras.

Lastly (I hope), at 5:00 a.m., I have to ask myself if I could have avoided this, even with the "whistleblower" history.

Did I not spend untold hours on the internet reading what some computer program at NSA might deem questionable? Did I not say much more than I should have on cell phones? Was all this recorded and catalogued and profiled? Of course.

Why? I know not, exactly. Still, I think of a friend's comment from years earlier: "Your Irish ancestry makes you have to fight oppression. After 800 years of dealing with British oppression, fighting oppression and subjugation becomes part of your genetic make-up." I have Jewish heritage, too. Enough to have me sent to Auschwitz quickly.

Evening.

Yesterday, we went to a nearby university to hear the wonderful Ruby Sales speak. On the way up, my wife said she needed about thirty minutes of research at the library.

"Do you really have to?" I queried. In all honesty, I was not eager to visit their library. The past several times there were police SUV's parked near our car, just an amazing coincidence that had not happened in the scores of times over the ten years that we had visited the library.

"Yes. I want to look up something."

I didn't argue. Our own internet was being well-monitored.

"I'll let you off at the door, then, and I'll just go through the mail." We had just picked up a pound of junk mail from our mailbox.

I found space in the shade and began reading mail. Within two or three minutes, the first SUV police wagon pulled in and parked. In another minute, another SUV wagon was there. It too parked.

I read the mail. Actually, I saw black on white letters and nothing more. My heart beat erratically, but forcefully. This had been the pattern for four weeks now. The day after I realized I was nuclear dead. The day I screamed out, "I might be dead, but I will take this to the ACLU and see if we can file a one point two billion dollar suit—all proceeds going to the ACLU to fight for freedom."

At that moment, I had no idea their surveillance probably covered our kitchen, our grand room, our bathroom, and especially our bedroom. The next day, I knew. A Palestinian driving a new Corvette down the Gaza Strip would not have gotten the police "protection" that I got. Then, the next day, and the next, for a month. From Tennessee to New England (especially New England!!??).

I sat, immobile—looking at black marks on white junk mail. For thirty minutes. A young woman had pulled in beside me in a new SUV! She didn't get out. She talked on her cell phone—for almost thirty minutes. Then, an angel came down the walkway. A little cherub Cherubini. She passed the police cruisers. "So very tough through everything," I thought. Her equanimity through witch trials was all that had saved me—many times.

Then, she was gone.

The police wagons were still there, but she was nowhere.

From my car seat, I could see nothing, except a small moving blob on the ground.

It couldn't be . . . yes, it was my wife of forty-two years. Seventy years old, crawling on the ground.

I should have been able to move to help her. I could not. Never in my own seventy years had I been so paralyzed. Not from fear, but in total revulsion. The lone woman on the phone pulled out and off hurriedly.

By the time I was out of the car and reaching out to her, she was on her feet. Barely, she could hardly stand, much less move. I didn't glance at the SUV's. I'm sure if they had seen a seventy year old woman crawling on the ground, they would have offered some assistance.

Somewhere in childhood, I had learned that that is what police are supposed to do. Or maybe the campus police don't worry about such small matters. She eased into the car. I trembled and felt sick. We didn't talk about it.

As we drove to the School of Theology auditorium, I did a "prayer" of my own type that Ruby Sales would say *something* that would make this fiasco trip worthwhile.

Something worthwhile turned into ninety minutes of greatness. A prevalent theme was that the struggle for equal treatment and justice is not over by any means. There was plenty of talk about the very country on planet earth that had to have, far and away, the highest incarceration rate.

We stood and joined hands and sang the old songs.
My wife was able to stand—even with an ankle already looking several times its normal size.

Still, we were swaying and smiling and singing for the first time in much more than thirty days.

And when mention was made that two out of three people in the world were those of color, I felt a bit more secure—for a few seconds.

My mind raced on fast forward to predator drones, spy drones, x-ray helicopters, nuclear submarines and drones, missiles and jets of every size carrying nuclear warheads. Chemical and biological warfare. And what of HAARP? What else is on the high tech horizon? We may not want to know.

Could a country the size of Lichtenstein, even, erase eight billion humans from the face of the earth with high tech weaponry?

We must think: at the time that 114 million Native

Americans and seventy-five million African Americans were genocidally murdered, there were no drones, no HAARP, no nuclear, almost no bio/chem weaponry, and no x-ray helicopters. There were antiquated guns, bludgeons, rope, and plenty of hatred.

The mountain road home was torturous. We wondered how many Ruby Sales it would take to sway a world.

October 11, 2013

Friday morning.

I went to bed last night thinking of the ever-present and relevant theme: my wife and I up against all the cloak and dagger agencies in America? And we don't know why. They semi-covertly trail and tail from Tennessee to Maine and New Hampshire, but nothing is explained. I'm guessing they have their reasons. And not good ones.

I read before sleeping, often back issues of magazines that have in-depth research. I have a stack of unread The Sun magazines, and randomly picked up a May 2003 issue. The very first article was entitled, "Tricks of the Trade, Alfred McCoy on How the CIA Got Involved in Global Drug Trafficking," by Derrick Jansen. Most of the long eleven page article is a Jensen interview with McCoy.

I read horrifying sentence after horrifying sentence. I won't attempt to summarize or paraphrase any of this article. What I would plead is that concerned Americans read this expose in the May 2003 copy of The Sun, published in Chapel Hill, N.C., or Alfred McCoy's book: Politics of Heroin: CIA Complicity in the Global Drug Trade.

I hope other readers will not feel the disgust and hopelessness I experienced.

For my part, I don't know who had the helicopters hovering over my house or why, but I would surmise a powerful government agency. Actually, several powerful government agencies, interconnected, and rolling in all the power and money the "Patriot" Act and the American tax payer can give them.

Again, no single individual can hope to survive

against these governmental powers. They have media, money, and expert manpower in every area they like. Whether it's surveillance, electronics, bombs and explosives, arson, chemicals bio terror germs, or quick murder, they have thousands of the most skilled operatives in the world.

And the top brass doesn't like critics or whistleblowers of any kind. Still, I keep thinking that: if "they" can badger/murder two educators with doctorates who have lived fairly squeaky clean lives, won innumerable awards, honors, and accolades, have degrees from top schools including the University of Virginia, Wake Forest, Auburn University, and a Harvard fellowship, dozens of years of working with young students for literary and sports events, who out there is safe? The answer has to be—practically no one!

I often trust my senses and intuition. Both keep telling me that what my wife and I are experiencing is part of a bit deeper south connection, with roots going back seventeen years.

October 13, 2013

Sunday.

Spent about one and one half hours at a studio gallery yesterday. I alluded to one fellow in his studio about our unbelievable and seemingly hopeless situation. His response sounded as if he had read a page from this diary: "They have unlimited resources."

I'm almost certain I have used that exact phrasing more than once in these pages because it is so manifest. What can stop a force that for no reason sends large black helicopters with x-ray machinery to sit on one's roof? Or to command a "covert" escort from Tennessee to Maine and back?

My wonder is why they are bothering with all the display of surveillance if they know their objective: whistleblower termination. But why am I still here? My guess would be that they have a neater set-up in the near future—one that will skewer me better and make their agencies look like saviors. If they can pull off presidential assassinations and destruction of huge buildings to start wars, they will do anything.

After all, did many Americans really care that our own CIA and other "allies" were complicit in heroin trafficking? From all that I have read, it seems that nothing—absolutely **nothing**—is too evil or horrible for "them" to take part in. Making certain that inner city youth have access to drugs as horrible as heroin or cocaine seems as bad to me as simply sending drones in and murdering people outright.

I am writing fast, and a bit nervously. It's almost like I could have them reading over my shoulder. Several sources have said they can—from over a mile high—

see everything you write. Through the roof.

Anyway, I'm thinking that I mentioned the fire in Town X about three weeks ago, just two houses down from my own riverfront house that we have had on the market for a few months. Just internet, not a realtor.

The house that burned had been on the market by a realtor/owner for many, many years that we know of. Neighbors were quick to ascertain the probable cause. ("It's insured . . . ," I heard someone say.)

The timing of the fire is what kept nagging at my mind. I had pulled out of my own driveway and driven past the house in question. I didn't glance at it; I hardly ever look at it.

After going by to pick up the mail and quickly check my mom's house, I returned to our riverfront house. Five to ten minutes plus another five to ten minutes for travel. Ten to twenty minutes total.

I had not planned to return to our house, but I couldn't recall whether I had reset the HVAC or locked the front door, even though I was pretty sure I had. Still, it was only a few blocks out of the way, and I decided to check.

When I got to my own street, I saw what I thought was a hazy leaf or turf dust in front of the house, but there was an elderly woman running down the drive with a broom.

I could tell it was smoke as I went by, and saw her coming back. I parked and walked quickly to where some of the neighbors were standing. They said they had contacted the fire department and the owner/realtor, who had been working in the house shortly before.

I stood around talking for a few minutes, wondering how long it would take a fire truck to get there. Finally, I went back to the house, sat down for a while, then went to the   window   to see if a fire truck had arrived. Nothing.

It took another ten minutes for the fire truck to arrive. The house was smoking badly. Never before had I realized how long it takes to prepare to fight a fire. That timing surprised me, too.   Still, I thought the firefighters were doing the best they could do. Quite a while later, another truck came by.   The timing kept nagging. Sheer coincidence? Possibly.

But yesterday morning, still in bed, I thought about our activity at the Town Y house *before* I went to Town X. We were, indeed, worried about helicopters taking pictures of possibly every piece of jewelry to every bit of cash we had in our safe. (With practically no bank interest out there, and a shaky bank situation for a decade or so, we have opted to keep most of our meager monetary assets in cash.)

We sat and talked about what we would do—right beside a huge wall window in the kitchen. Take several thousands and put it in the "secret closet." If there were a surveillance mike aimed at the house that window would probably be the most likely. There would have been more than ninety minutes for someone to set the scene.

I have no idea if a connection like that was part of their plan. But after living in South Georgia, I learned that fire is still an effective tool for the devious. The most obvious being the burning of a large house that an African American family had bought in a white neighborhood.

In our final few months in South Georgia, I was up at daybreak to put the coffee on. I smelled something electrical—burning. I looked inside the cabinets and around the electrical outlets. Nothing. But the smell was not abating. I called someone I might trust and who had a good knowledge of electrical matters. He was there in just one or two minutes and was more upset than I was. He went through all the cabinets and said he'd better get a working electrician—one that I also knew. They were both at the house within several minutes. The electrician knew where to look—a broom closet. He called me to look. A wire coming from under the house touched the flooring. Nice old heart pine flooring. Heart pine, I knew, was used as a fire starter. Where the wire touched the floor, an orange glow, the size of a quarter, emanated. The electrician quickly remedied matters, and pulled out the entire section of wire. Silently, he held up the wire. We shook our heads, in silence. Finally, I said something about "old wiring." They nodded. At that moment, I thought, "accident." It was much later that I became certain it was not an accident from old wiring.

It took only seconds for me to decide that the house for sale two houses from our river house was no accident, either. I thought: "They" can do—and will do—anything. Expertise—the best in the world—for explosions, for murders and assassinations, for drug trafficking, for covert surveillance, for propaganda and character smears, for tactics reminiscent of the Gestapo, for fires and wars, and so much more. Then, I remembered reading one short, simple sentence: "Fires can be started using satellite technology." (Paul Baird)

October 16, 2013

Wednesday.

Getting up half an hour early had probably saved the house—possibly our lives. It was some weeks later that I thought more about the incident. I'd never had a fire problem in fifty-two years, but that was the scariest time we had experienced in that county, and the wire in question was rather **neatly frayed.** Something had looked unnaturally clean about the fray. Then, there was the history. Not only in that county.

Two days ago, I found a book in a sale room at the library. (I'm not checking out books or using the internet or pertinent calls for information any more.) The book is entitled Buried in the Bitter Waters: The Hidden History of Racial Cleansing in America by Elliot Jaspin, 2007.

Jaspin carefully documents reductions—some very great—of African American populations, mostly in the South. He calls the tables listed just a sampling, and this reader got the impression that the much larger truth is indeed, "buried in bitter waters."

Back to the house that recently burned. While I had nothing whatsoever to gain, had the fire spread, I could possibly have lost tens of thousands of dollars worth of uninsured musical instruments. Just **one** guitar, the one I played in college, was recently appraised at thirty-five thousand.

I mention all this not just because of the fire's timing, but because the police "presence" increased sharply the next day and for several weeks thereafter. (This increased presence was on top of the increase the day after I brashly declared we would sue Homeland Security for $1.2 billion.) A little paranoia and conjecture?

I hoped so, but in my near seventy years, I had never seen so many bizarre "coincidences."

Try to imagine a seventy year old doctor running across a neighbor's back yard in bright daylight to start a fire in a house he has never been in and which has been on the market for about a decade. My house is fully furnished. I could have spent the night and done a dastardly deed under cover of night. But that kind of evil is what the chaos, confusion, and civil strife guys live for, not me. Though I am someone who has nothing to gain, I imagine *someone* might have had much to gain. An agency?

But do the government agencies with **unlimited resources** care? Not a whit. Trayvon is only one example (but a prime example) of possibly millions of cases of justice run amuck in America.

Also in the library was a Harper's magazine with an intriguing title: "Life as a Terrorist: Uncovering My FBI File," by William T. Vollmann. Just last month's issue (September, 2013).

As I read the article, I kept thinking how horrible his experience was. Long after finishing, I realized that his experience with government agents could have been a picnic in the park compared to what I might be experiencing. His was mostly before the "Patriot" Act was enacted. Before the Bush/Obama hard surveillance. Before ubiquitous cell phone use. Still, his ordeal was horrible. This article is one that any American who feels secure about what his government is doing should read. Please take twenty minutes of time to at least scan it. Then, think about my situation in the here and now of 2013: Horrible! Overwhelming! Hopeless . . . ?

But I keep writing. My wife and I don't talk much

since we are almost certain the house, the cars, and even the outdoors are all part of their surveillance. Overnight, you stop saying things like: "Damn, that was wonderful love making, wasn't it!"

When you're positive that the "spooks" (Vollmann, too, thinks that word is appropriate) are recording every one of your most private words, most conversation, and many other normal activities, you become guarded for a while. Then, even the words stop. Something as natural as, say, flatulence, in your own living room, becomes a source of doubt—and fear. Could they make a case out of that gas expulsion!? Recall the rat experiments. *We* are the *rats*.

For a professional writer like Vollmann, writing is likely a natural activity. For me, speaking is natural. Writing is too often a chore and a bit of trouble. But within a few weeks, it has become the preferred medium. Any private matters are extremely awkward for us. We sit on the couch away from the suspect window and cover ourselves with a large, three inch thick, piece of foam. Then, we try to whisper in each other's ear.

What is that secretive? Nothing much, really. But it's like phone use and the internet. You don't necessarily want someone who is trying to harm you knowing your every thought! Still, even with the foam, I feel as if their high tech mikes are hearing every word.

Gertrude Stein said that nineteenth century people saw parts of things and tried to create a whole. Like my dear ninety-three year old mother, who has little to do all day except watch the neighbors. If she sees too many cars going to a residence, she knows they are selling or making drugs. If she sees a guy home during the week, he's been fired or laid off. If she sees an animated conversation between husband and wife, they are probably about to divorce. Almost every day, there is a new, and absurd, construct. These tales remind me a lot of the government agency constructs that William T. Vollmann had to deal with.

I strongly believe that profiling is akin to voodoo psychology, and that agencies are overusing and not understanding the limits of that voodoo. Whether it's racial, religious, ethnic, national, or whatever—it's voodoo.

Further, I emphatically believe that there are very few statements that can be judged without *a full contextual basis.* Not a phrase here or a paragraph there in an email or phone conversation, but the complete contextual basis. This opinion is as much drawn from common sense as it is from a quarter of a century of teaching communications.

A background search that goes back to early childhood, with intent to profile, could certainly be an easy task for your government agency profiler. Especially if they have unlimited resources. Even before I became a "whistleblower" of sorts, I knew of a host of people who would relish an opportunity to nail me to a cross. Colleagues at work, jealous friends, jealous enemies. I think most everyone has a few. But if you've enraged a goodly percent of a nation by exposing civil rights violations, expect hell on earth. I have spent more time in the deep south than anywhere else. I should know.

October 18, 2013

Friday.

I have always had very little respect for eavesdroppers, spies, night watchers, rapists, and murderers.

I remember, as a youngster in the early 1950's, the old "party line" telephone connections. Neighbors, or maybe someone across town, could pick up their phone and listen to your phone conversation. Most of the time the picker-upper would put his phone down and give you time to finish your conversation. But some people on some of the party lines would not hang up. They would listen to anyone's conversation at any time. Better than TV, I suppose. Callers, sensing someone was eavesdropping, would get angry. Enraged—sometimes rabid, and would scream things like: "Hang up the goddamn phone, asshole. If I find out who you are, I'll …"

That was how people in the 50's felt about privacy. Now, no one much seems to care: "Yeah, I guess my life's an open book, huh?" If they really knew how open! *And how dangerous open can be.*

But then, there have to be a few throwbacks to the 50's. Like me, I admit. For quite some years, I have detested the thought of eavesdroppers listening in, and recording, *forever*! I still think of wiretapping as a serious Watergate issue. But possibly such unwarranted "listening" is something only the very powerful can get away with or take issue with.

For my part, I often try to "entertain" the eavesdroppers if the conversation gets boring. I have entertained with exciting fictional accounts. I've entertained with sexy stories. And sexism. And sometimes pent up feelings about NSA, CIA, and the Super Security guys. I have deliberately lambasted most everyone—often to entertain the eavesdroppers!

Did they appreciate it? Only now do I realize they really have been listening. Carefully. So, I've put my life on the line. Again,

> 24/7/365 surveillance in every room and vehicle is hardly privacy.
> "The ninth and tenth amendments were included to make sure there was absolutely no misunderstanding about the limited powers the Constitution grants to the federal government. . . . The government has no power to tell the people what to do except in areas specifically authorized in the Constitution."
> —Harry Browne
> From "The Constitution and the Right to Privacy"
> tenthamendmentcenter.com

and today I read where it's only going to get worse. RFID chips? Spy drones everywhere? Mikes and cameras in every room? Of course. And so much more. Technology always breeds higher technology. Geeks around the world are, this minute, devising better ways to spy on us. I think of the rat experiments. I think, too, that the people who control the recorded information (phone calls and computer searches) also control the world and, ultimately the history of our world. They can very arbitrarily and deliberately release or suppress (or delete) whatever they like.

So, they have their pieces of fiction from the last two decades.

"Okay, men, let's turn this from talk to action. We've got all the experts, and we've got money to buy anything and everyone we need."

The day I began this diary was the very day that a connection between eczema and helicopters occurred to me. For minutes, I was in disbelief and near shock. I remember walking around the kitchen shaking my head, telling my wife I would write a daily account, sue for one point two billion, and have the amount go for civil rights work. I was blustery, my ire adding a few decibels in an otherwise quiet kitchen. (I didn't know then that you cannot sue most of these agencies!?)

The very next day, and for many other days, the squad cars were around me, like a swarm of yellow jackets. Sort of "covert," but more cars than in any one day in my life. They were smooth, and there have been no stops, but one gets concerned. Then, after a week or so, they dropped off to almost normal.

Ten days later, we decided that I should take some

of the valuables to the river house, since I was scheduled to drive to New England in two days. We were still the nervous about an x-ray copter probably knowing where things were better than we did. We talked and prepared in kitchen again. The timing of the fire. The timing of the "covert" squad cars. The kitchen! It took until several days ago to make the connection. The kitchen very likely was bugged or miked—possibly from the woods behind. I may be conjecturing, and I'm certainly a bit stressed lately. But I've read the espionage genre enough to know about coincidences. They don't happen.

Each day I'm more ill at ease. Experts with unlimited resources and the face of the law, are, simply, going to succeed. Their operatives may have had experience in starting entire wars in third world countries. Or drug trafficking or political assassinations. Or revolutions, or total chaos and confusion all over the world. I told my wife we are about as powerful as a gnat or an ant perched on the kitchen counter. "They" have the power and expertise to create **any** kind of setup and have me (or you) convicted.

A quote from the book, Spychips, by Katherine Albrecht and Liz McIntyre, 2005.

"No matter how much you trust your government, giving it unchecked ability to observe and control your life is like putting a noose around your neck and hoping the guy on the other end never pulls the rope.

You might think you're handing that rope to Mother Teresa only to find yourself one day staring into the eyes of . . . Adolph Hitler." (p. 212)

And one more quote from the same source:

"Hundreds of millions of people have been slaughtered in cold blood by the very authorities that were supposed to be in charge of protecting them." (p. 212)

October 21, 2013

Monday.

I am sickened to the point of tears when I think of my wife's part in this nightmare. It's not just her fall and the resulting sprained ankle at the college library, nor is it the losing of her cell phone or other obvious manifestations of the stress. It is the haunted, haggard, overstressed, and . . . fearful look on her face.

Although both of her siblings died of Alzheimer's much younger than she is now, she, at seventy, has thus far exhibited none of the signs. She has eaten mostly organic whole foods, exercised on a regular basis, and has kept her mind as young and active as any seventy or forty year old I have ever heard of. She even reads a best selling novel every four to seven days, usually.

I have been worried for two months. Very worried, knowing that stress can be a major trigger of Alzheimer's onset. She has been concerned, too, but careful not to mention it until a couple of days ago. She approached the subject obliquely, asking me if I thought her relative's cancer might have been brought on by family stress.

I said it probably did not help, but asked if she had been thinking of her own situation?

"Of course. Many times each day."

My own mind wanted to go catatonic.

You think about how many forces the government agencies control (millions with unlimited money and expertise), and you marvel that you are still alive—sort of. You scratch and poke your skin to make certain there is still feeling.

I look again at my wife across the room: silent,

numb. And I tell myself it is natural, it is the way you become when you know every move you make, including your trips to the bathroom, is being recorded.

Lively political discussions/arguments are a thing of the past. Probably forever. I recall that "The Companies" never relent. I recall the many writers who have said that Hitler would have been in Nazi heaven if he had had the kind of surveillance our government has at this moment.

I awoke at 12:15 this morning in the middle of a colorless, plotless dream. One that could have been a black and white "Hopper." Within moments, my mind had jumped back eight years to a poem I had written. I think the title was "Trust Your Dog." The poem described my dog's behavior when I took her for her 9:30 or 10:00 P.M. outings. Every so often (sometimes twice a week, sometimes twice a month), she would dance back and forth, sideways, as if on air. A breeder/trainer had shown me that such movement is how this breed reacts to a strange *human* in the vicinity. Never for an animal. Squirrels or cats, they go straight for.

My Angel was telling about a night watcher, or night stalker, I believed. I would stare into the deep woods where the dog was focused. Nothing. But then, my night vision isn't the world's best.

I tried bright beam lights several times. I tried talking. I told the stalker I was going to unleash my dog the next time. Eventually, he would find out that was not true, but for a month or so, there was no dog dance. Then, the dances resumed for many more months, sometimes nightly.

One night, after our showers, I said, let's take the dog out again. We'd already done the final outing for the evening, so if there were a stalker, I thought we might catch him off guard. But the dog heard nothing.

A few nights later though, our dog was in the air, soon followed by her low growling, then the bark. Human, not animal, I thought, even though we could see nothing. But I felt the stalker could. Several more times we tried, but there was nothing. Our dog no longer found it necessary to warn us.

Incidentally, our house is totally invisible, even in daylight. The nearest neighbors are quite some distance, and thick hedges and bushes make the lot very private, even in daylight.

If there really were a watcher, we never heard. And I'm not sure why this seemed important at midnight. I hadn't thought about it in months, maybe years. But . . . this was likely a prelude to the intrusion that would carry on for many years.

So, why do I care enough to jot all this down? At seventy years of age, a future begins to look a lot smaller. But when I see throngs of youth that deserve the best, I wonder more and more how they will survive in the new technocracy.

As late afternoon encroaches, I feel more despondent, and wonder what revelation midnight might bring.

October 25, 2013

Friday.

Just four days have elapsed, but it seems like months.

Health. My wife is doing a bit better with a new ankle brace. I am doing worse on the internal organ situation. Yesterday, at my mom's house, I could hardly stand the pain as I talked. I had to keep pushing on my stomach to bear it. She noticed. "Get to a doctor," she said. Today is just as bad.

We tried to find an NAACP office in Huntsville. Went to the only listed Church Street. It was in Madison, AL. After inquiry, a lady said there was a Church Street in downtown Huntsville. Finally, we found the office. It's only open on Monday. We were intent on donating a sizable amount (for us) because if something happens, anything we have will likely go into agency/government/criminal hands. Their power is phenomenal.

On the way back from Madison to Huntsville, we passed an electronic surveillance shop. I pulled in just beyond it and we walked back. I was interested in a "sweeper" to see if they had our cars and house and yard bugged as I assumed they were.

The young guy was most helpful. He'd sold his last sweeper yesterday afternoon. "Everyone is getting them," he said, but we talked. He said a sweeper was *no* good for the new laser bugs; only some kind of "iron dome," which he did not sell, worked on the lasers. "Lasers are what law enforcement uses," he told us. But he went on to say that you could tell, using a cell phone camera, if a laser was aimed at you. He also said that law enforcement needed a judge's order to use the laser because they tracked every single thing you did. He as much as said anyone who wants the judge's order gets it (I had already read that), and that THEY can do *anything*! (My first comment when I realized I had been nuked.)

Did I mention the dead raccoon by the mailbox? It took me twenty minutes to see a possible racial comment. The city did *not* pick it up, even though we had called. We had to remove it. It had rotted and smelled beyond belief. It was the first such dead animal in our yard in over three decades. The last was a possum on Halloween night left by a nasty student. It made me wonder about the mentality of . . . whoever we were being plagued by and their totally tasteless acts of terrorism. But *they*—in all their deviousness—will likely destroy us. Unlimited resources and too many practice sessions to fathom—around the globe, probably. Also, wondering if all this work and money spent on ruining us is their way of showing the world what happens when you "blow a whistle." You are going to get hurt—bad!

October 26, 2013

Saturday.

Little sleep last night. (Three hours.) Just a racing mind. I kept trying deep, slow breathing and meditation, but it still did not really help.

What should be nothing to ever worry about popped into mind. I thought about the Vollmann article and how the Agency took a friend's copy of <u>Lolita</u> as possible evidence of his being a child pornographer, when actually, he was a museum quality photographer. I thought about my many hundreds of books, many of which deal with political dissent, and thought of what they could make up about that. Then, I thought about other things, like my eight vehicles, four lawn tractors, three chain saws, two weed whackers, three self-propelled mowers, and two gas leaf blowers. Twenty-two vehicles and gas engine work tools. They all use gas or a gas/oil mix. For almost three long seasons, they are used regularly, and a pretty fair amount of gas goes through them. Before I burned out three pieces of equipment, I was using *any* gas. The mechanics kept saying, "Dump your gas out after three weeks!" I didn't, and things kept breaking down, including a newer car engine. I finally got the message. Don't use ethanol gas, especially in small engines.

I have used real gas for several years now and had great success. Cars, too. Then, two of the three stations that I bought non-ethanol gas from went out of business or stopped selling it. I talked with them, and they were truly sorry. Both had the story that pure gas was being forced out. Tractor Supply had gas cans for $5.00. I bought about ten, just in case. I half filled several of them, but I had the others if it appeared that a phase out was occurring. However, pure gas didn't phase out in this area, and I even found a few other venues. I still have a dozen or so cans—perfectly legal *and sensible* with a dozen pieces of lawn equipment, or even in the event of a crisis. Recall the New York and New Jersey storms and how people were using milk jugs and glass containers to transport fuel. Water, food, and fuel are a large part of emergency preparedness.

When I'm mowing, I always leave the shed or garage doors open. Nothing to hide. But if a <u>Lolita</u> novel can help to frame a case, well, most anything out there could be used.

The raccoon and a blown computer a week ago ($200 repair) are nerve wracking nuisances bordering on *terrorism*, as is the flurry of "covert" police presence in ten states. What chills me is the fire.

The fire occurred between the homes of two quite elderly ladies, both of whom I happen to like very much as they are always friendly and down to earth. The kind of people who would deliberately (?) start a fire in such close proximity to these women, possibly to implicate a whistleblower (!?), would do anything. Any deed as dastardly as it might get—including, making certain our inner cities, often ghettoes, are filled with hard drugs. I get both sick and angry thinking about it.

They can nuke us from a huge Chinook helicopter, sabotage anything out there, start civil strife and wars, and create more chaos and confusion than anyone in world ever dreamed of—including Hitler!

These agencies now have super high technology at their fingertips, and a host of nuclear, chemical laser, and biological options. Not   to   forget, unlimited funding. They tell Congress how   much   money they need, and they get it, quite unlike any worthwhile charity. These inhuman types have had sixty inventive years to improve upon Hitler's archaic, but still effective, systems of murder.

I have read enough political intrigue to realize these inhuman types keep you in their sights.

Do I sit around and wait for their next severe terrorist act, or maybe a fire that kills someone, or an explosion, or the semi-truck "accident" that will take our lives, or maybe just implicate very well. They have thousands of tricks that the most devious minds in the world can create.

I want *none* of it. This is not the America I knew for my first sixty years. I am appalled.

October 27, 2013

Sunday morning, and most of the horror thoughts from 2:00 until 7:00 A.M. are gone, for the moment. No, not gone, just less vivid. The recurring nightmare thought is—if this group (or someone) would start a house fire, they would do anything. ANYTHING! Actually, this same thought entered my mind, only seconds after I connected the hovering helicopters with my eczema.

They could kill me much more quickly. So what could be the advantage in the long/painful death or setting up a house fire case? The joy of showing they can easily rig a case? Or sitting back and waiting for the experienced "pros" to devise a far tighter setup than the previous? I don't know.

Having already mentioned that I "almost purposely" said quite a few things that might irk an eavesdropper from NSA, I keep thinking of new comments that might have provoked. The following were to my ninety-three year old mother or my seventy year old wife:

♦Homeland Security gets all the money it wants while health care and social programs are being cut.

♦Our special forces are out there in about fifty or sixty countries creating chaos and confusion, wars and civil strife.

♦The CIA is complicit in assassination and much more, I believe.

These statements came from many of the books I have or from the internet. I can't prove any of them, and I don't think I needed to, in talking with my ninety-three year old, home-bound mother. And like most Americans, including many attorneys, I haven't had a chance to read all of the "Patriot" Act. And I'm sure if we had read it, we still wouldn't understand the exact implications.

Still, I really am sorry for making any unfounded comments to my ninety-three year old mom—and those others listening in on what I thought might be a private conversation.

> **"Discrediting is a very easy matter when those with evil intent control your movement, speech, behavior—in other words, your entire mind."**
>
> —Dr. "C"

I thought about aforementioned racist and sexist comments. YUK! I must be human. I'm not perfect, after all. But then I have never gotten to know *anyone* well who didn't have at least a fleeting prejudicial moment. No one—ever. Yet, most were good people whose public actions would never hurt anyone. Fairly recently, an Indian student/scholar was telling me how Ghandi, even, had racist moments. My esteem for Ghandi did not waver for a second. First, I knew of him as a real human being, not a mythological god. Second, I think we can pardon any fleeting prejudice from a man who devoted his entire life to humankind.

Still, it would be nice to be a perfect saint. And I regret many comments. Even more, I regret private comments made public—twisted out of context. I read in Forty Ways to Raise a Non-racist Child (Mathias and French), "Face it. Race-based discrimination is as American as apple pie." But their point, and mine, is that people must know and admit their prejudices before their energies can be used to overcome them. Not just in America; the world over.

Too, my thoughts often go back to the HAARP technology. Could they, or ELF waves have been bombarding for two decades or so? Not one bit less possible than getting x-rayed from a copter. I think about my language, and it's almost another, totally different person. HAARP? Maybe.

Just as likely is a phenomenon similar to the one that writer/researcher Michelle Alexander speaks about: the system's demeaning of African Americans by our own government/society. Always the drug association, so they can be incarcerated, or worse. Ms. Alexander is well worth reading.

Every time I get on the internet, I am struck with "Breaking News" headlines. What is most striking is that the greatest part of "news" that concerns Black Americans is which rap artist just got busted for drugs. Or a sports item. I believe there should be better news. After all, we have, as a society, murdered/killed more than seventy-five million African Americans by some estimates. This is one sickening legacy.

That said, again, the horror thoughts never leave me. I am likely being "slow deathed" by the world's masters of evil. I have read the books (often, *they* are portrayed as the "good guys") telling how they have skills to do anything and everything dastardly and deathly. They have all the resources that *our tax dollars* can possibly buy them.

One final word about NSA/CIA and any others who have access to phone/internet/surveillance: we might have several prejudicial comments over decades that they can pull up and make quite a stir about. There may be hundreds or thousands of comments that run counter, but these comments will never be heard. They will be ignored or deleted—lost. With such power, the NSA/CIA can control the very history of America—and even the world.

October 28, 2013

Monday.

Awoke at 4:00 A.M., and for my first cup of coffee, I was feeling okay. By the second cup, I was again feeling the weight of what we were likely up against.

I finally looked up something relevant on the internet—Mind Control—in between a number of mundane topics. It took quite a while for HAARP to appear, but as I read a couple entries, I was thinking that the fellow in New England was correct. I wonder how long ago this could have begun, possibly shortly after (or even before) I retired. If the technology is out there (like surveillance electronics), they're going to find someone to use it and someone to use it on.

Still, I don't think of what I did as "blowing a whistle." I did what I did because I wanted to be fair, just, and legal.

The weight of it all dampens my spirit, today. I have given much thought to it. One individual couple cannot hope to survive the combined forces out there, all working together as they should if their work were really for the *right* thing. But it is *NOT!*

The town police and the highway troopers get a directive from above, and they do their jobs. We have just witnessed, as a country, what happens to the Snowdens, *et al.,* of America who put their lives on the line to warn us of highly questionable practices.

I hate to think about the future. Where and when will they set the next fire?? Who could be hurt or killed? Chances are excellent, too, that they won't be quite as hasty and sloppy and absurd in the next one. These really are chaos and civil strife professionals, most of the time.

It is really hard to believe I am seeing this. It's even harder to believe that I am part of it.

October 29, 2013

Radiation on . . . My Pillow?

Shortly after 9/11, we went into our emergency preparedness phase . . . again. We had done something like that in the 80's after reading a Howard Ruff book.

We stocked the shelves with enough food to last for many weeks, if not months. Twenty or so gallons of pure water in the garage. Extra vehicle fuel. A new camp stove. Extra ammo in case of "invasion." More blankets, candles, duct tape, silver coins, etc. You've no doubt read the emergency survival guidelines.

I even went so far as to buy a radiation detector (ten years before Fukushima). After connecting the black helicopters (and radiation) with my severe eczema, I was curious to see if anything in the house might contain enough radiation to register on the detector. (At no time did the Fukushima radiation ever make a noticeable difference.)

I checked for about twenty minutes and thought the old shotgun, inherited from my dad, might possibly be a bit higher. That might make sense if helicopter crews were x-raying for guns. (H-m-m-m. Everyone in the area seems to have guns—and not antique shotguns or .22's! But we didn't see helicopters hovering over their homes.)

Then, we went to the bedroom. Nothing until I got to the wall at the head of the bed. The activity "ticks" were suddenly many times greater.

"Good God!" I heard my wife gasp.

I, too, was nonplussed. Why right here near the pillows? I wondered. I put the detector close to my pillow, and it became even more excited . . . ticking nonstop.

"It's even higher on my pillow!" my wife gasped again.

I reminded her that our pillows get swapped regularly. But the point is—*radiation in or on the pillows!*

This was eight or nine weeks ago. We have not had time to research, or even think about, the implications. When we do (if we ever do), I doubt they will be pleasant.

November 17, 2013

Sunday.

More than two weeks since I stopped entries. Most of that time it seemed as if things might be improving. A state of normalcy around the corner.

Thursday (November 14), in fact, we sat in the kitchen talking about the CIA. The CIA. I asked my wife if she remembered the "You Tube" clip where the rear bumper guards were ordered to get off the bumper shortly before the assassination of President Kennedy. One of the guards obviously did *not* want to get off. It seems that he got yet another directive to dismount. He did, but he faced the man giving the order and seemed to offer an argument. The words remain unknown, but his body language showed that he was most upset at the order.

My wife remembered the clip. I told her that I would never forget the guard's outstretched arms—as if pleading to be able to do the job he was supposed to do. A dour stone face gave him no rationale. The bumper guard, in a state of disbelief, walked off. He had just expressed defiance in front of what would be many millions.

I mentioned, in the kitchen, that the guard was the one I would always remember and respect as an example of the best our Secret Service and law enforcement has to offer, and that, conceivably, ninety-five or even ninety-eight percent could be so dedicated. Their jobs, their futures, their lives—on the line to protect their people.

The next day was Friday, November 15. I won't forget it. We left to do some leaf raking at the lake cottage. We took the back road. A police cruiser, traveling in the opposite direction, went by us as we slowed for a stop sign. Automatically, I glanced in my mirror, surprised to see the cruiser turn into a farm driveway. I stopped and waited for several cars to pull off. I took a last look behind me and saw the cruiser back out and continue in the direction it had been going.

That entire move seemed odd. I wondered if I should expect something to happen in the lake house town.

Within ten minutes, I had forgotten about the incident.

Then, about a mile or so from my destination, a large Tahoe SUV coming in our direction suddenly turned directly in front of us. Only super quick seventy year old reflexes saved us, along with excellent brakes.

Inside several split seconds, I saw the front passenger door of the Tahoe inches from my bumper. Then, I saw the driver, mouth open, as if in shock. Then, I saw his arms open wide, as if in apology. I waved, saying okay, thanks for being sorry. I meant it.

Still, in over three million miles of driving, I have never had anyone turn directly in front of me like that. Within ten to fifteen seconds, I turned to my wife and asked if the Tahoe's sudden, inexplicable move was more conjecture or what.

Anyway, at least the Tahoe driver acted as if he were sorry—an open-mouthed, appalled expression, with arms outstretched.

With arms outstretched! It wasn't until the next morning that the outstretched arms took on another meaning: derisive mockery. The bumper guard with arms outstretched.

That morning I was tight-chested and sickened—again. They were having fun—murderous great fun. My wife was in the passenger seat, and the large SUV would have been unforgiving. I find it contrary to anything in nature that humans can be so murderous.

November 30, 2013

Ninety days after the first entry. I glanced over the previous sixty days or so, yesterday, and got disgusted. It is what it is: a haphazard reaction at being a prime CIA (or some agency) target. (I keep coming back to CIA because the patterns mentioned by Paul Baird, Jim Keith, Jim Marrs, James W. Douglass, Grant Jeffery, and Amy Goodman seem to mirror images of what we are experiencing. These are books from my personal library, since I have still refrained from using public libraries.)

As I tried to light edit, I became even more disappointed and tired. Ninety days of wondering what their next trick will be, or where the next fire will be, or who our assassin will be, and what method. After the extreme eczema, another assassin for me might be superfluous.

I would like to mention the last "pleasant" little trick. It was eight or nine days ago, but I didn't even note it on my calendar, it seemed so insignificant at the time. And, I'm getting very tired of it all.

But the incident: I was in a book store (still trying to find relevant materials on HAARP, microwave mind control, and electronic assault. Zilch in that bookstore). I was crouched, looking at a bottom shelf, when someone came by and stopped. I looked up into a huge smiling and friendly face.

He said, "Oh, man! I like your style. That's really cool." He pointed at my shoes and jacket, and his smile got bigger.

I stood up, saying, "Thanks! Are you from here in town?"

I didn't know what else to say. No stranger had ever been so friendly, complimentary, and smiling so big that

I could ever recall. Several red flags went up in my mind for some reason.

"I'm about an hour away in _____. "I just wanted to tell you how much I like your style." The smile never wavered as he pointed to my shoes and coat again.

"Okay. Thanks again, and take care," I said as I shook his extended hand, then watched him walk away.

I knew almost instantly that I had met one of "them." The reference to "really liking my style" came from an area a bit more than an hour from the School of the Americas. My teaching job was just seventy-five or eighty miles from that infamous school. The high schoolers I taught <u>loved</u> to tease me about dressing sharp. The guy who had just stopped did a perfect reenactment of what the kids had done quite a few times each year. And, yeah, I'd tease them back. This was bus duty or hall duty camaraderie—not during class!

I almost liked the guy in the bookstore for taking me back twenty years. (I do miss the kids!)

Still, almost three months of tricks (possibly eighteen or nineteen years of tricks that I didn't even recognize) have kept the red flags up. The book store incident was all too similar to another incident when a laughing, joking, friendly older guy came by to do work around the house—for free! I paid him anyway, and a few days later almost paid very, very dearly.

The significance of the bookstore event was to tell me that my old "friends" were still there . . . and that they had big connections. Yes, greater connections than I had ever dreamed. If the point hasn't already become redundant, I say it one more time to be certain: these agents and their millions of cohorts can do, and will do, anything! Anyone can do an internet search (except for me!) on government agency abuses and illegal activities and get a bigger picture, no doubt. But from my meager half dozen sources, let me list:

♦ Global drug trade complicity

♦ Mind control experimentation

♦ Unlimited resources (including experts in every field, such as, explosives; assassination; arson; wiretapping; internet, house, and car surveillance at all times; access to much, if not all the weaponry of the U. S. military; total cooperation of the military and all other law agencies; extreme media control; and general harassment experts.

♦ A "badge" that instills chilling fear, and even pandering respect.

This list is by no means all inclusive.

A few thoughts keep surfacing in my own mind that I simply have not included so far.

First, there is no doubt that a fairly large percentage of agents and all the other branches of local law enforcement officers are doing a great job and are as dedicated and honest as we might hope for. Unfortunately, many are all too human and choose to turn a blind eye and go along with an insanely corrupt and evil system. They have families and expenses and, of course, their own livelihood to worry about. Never before had I even thought about police not only having to worry about dangerous criminals—but even **more dangerous agencies** that could likely eliminate them instantly. For that reason, we are not going to see many whistleblowers or anyone raising an eyebrow to question. Knowing the fraught danger of a question, I have to wonder if I would be so bold. I would hope so, but I just don't know.

Which leads into another point: If I'm quite "under the gun" (read compromised or much worse), why am I even keeping these notes? Especially since, if "they" know, and "they" probably do, it could make matters worse?

I don't know. Possibly several reasons. One reason is to verify much of what writers like Marrs, Keith, Douglass, Jeffrey, and Baird have already noted. Then, too, the government agents have spread—I don't even know what kind of lies and twisted half-truths and insinuations about me (and possibly my wife). It would be nice to have the truthful side out there. "They" have never confronted me, and neither has anyone else. But word gets around fast, and it is easy, and heart rending, to see the flash of fear on a face that has always been friendly.

I doubt any of this will get published or even read. But the very act of writing has kept both of us going. I keep thinking of that diary by a thirteen year old in Holland, and my heart goes out for her more than ever. She was only thirteen. My wife and I are a few days more and a few days less than seventy. Anne Frank was fifty-seven years younger and prevented from fulfilling those fifty-seven years because of someone's "final solution"—*genocide*.

I keep coming back to the reasons for our situation. I've called it political. Yes. I've called it revenge by powerful people from another era. And, yes, that is possible, but government help would be necessary.

There were big black helicopters. I have never called it an error or a misunderstanding.

Most everyone in this area of origin would know better. Someone would know better. Someone would want to discuss or talk about it. They would have sense to know that a retired educator doesn't go mad at age seventy and do ludicrous, heinous acts that he would die, yes die, before doing at any other time in his sixty-nine years. But what about all the baloney/crap they have

Paul Baird has researched "surveillance" for more than two decades. He says, "The magnetic field around the head, the brain waves of an individual, can be monitored by satellite . . . the results . . . fed back to . . . computers. Eventually, they will monitor almost everyone."

on their recorders from twenty years of 24/7 spying on your houses, cars, and persons—wherever you might be?

Much, and **very** much of the past eight or nine years is, as stated above, pure crap. Rotten baloney. For their ears and eyes. I really dislike the very idea of **anyone** spying/stalking/watching us. But when innumerable coincidences occur, red flags go up. But you're never one hundred percent positive until the black helicopters hover over your roof, and at times, you wonder a bit if you've been suspicious for no reason.

Still, so certain, much of the time, and so irked at the idea, we staged many events and conversations for them. The more bizarre, the better, I felt. Ditto for the phone conversations and computer searches. Quite a few times, I wrote out scripts. We did enactments of . . . anything and everything. If they were watching, they might show themselves.

But they never showed. Our doubts and charades continued. I assumed our watchers would be locals—out to get some things to gossip about. I wasn't expecting what could be—the world's most dangerous and powerful covert organizations!

I have thus far only alluded to what it is. After ninety long, horrible days of thought and writing, I see it all as genocide. I sensed from the first black helicopter over my house, it was genocide. And eugenics.

Even in the earliest days of dealing with hard racial tracking, new articles, and a few concerned people, kept mentioning that white men just don't try to remedy civil rights abuses. And locally, they impressed that point well—amazingly well, considering they didn't have the unlimited resources and manpower of the government agencies.

Early in the Bush era, I learned that you didn't mention your past work as a "whistleblower" to anyone. So often, such comments would be met with a stone cold stare and conversation would cease.

The message was clear. One does not transgress or dismantle any of the racial barriers society has erected.

A burgeoning prison industry in America and wholesale incarceration of African American males keeps the barriers in place. As does drug trafficking and even many aspects of our education system.

Yes, if one meddles with the system, he/she will be murdered, at best. Or forever tormented/tortured. To me, that is worse.

In this final analysis, I had hoped to have more research about electronic assault and mind control and HAARP and microwave assaults. For obvious reasons, I am not researching these topics on the internet yet. But, I firmly believe that I have been the victim of electronic assault for a dozen years or so. With the discovery of "bugs" in three of my vehicles, there was no doubt we were under surveillance, and the Paul Baird article points out, "Those under surveillance [can be] used for remote experimentation." (I am against using dogs, cats, and even rabbits for experimentation, much less humans— U. S. citizens, at that!)

The very subtitle of the Baird article says: Victims can experience hearing voices, mind reading, directed energy attacks, and more.

Clearly, this is the area that may be more conjectural and harder to prove. Indeed, Jim Keith points out in his 1999 book on mass control that a chief advantage of directed energy systems is the *deniability* factor. No bullet holes, no fragmentation, no trace of poisons.

Whether or not I was the victim of electronic assault, I simply want others to know what can happen if one speaks out or takes action against oppression. Much of the material here is as concrete as seeing a helicopter over your roof. Some is trying to convey your emotions when you are fairly certain people are playing deadly games. Some is still conjecture, of course. So why not conjecture a bit further. HAARP, ELF, and microwave electronic assault weapons are not new technology. Their deadly power is not even in the same realm as talking to green aliens from UFO's. Still, the absence of concrete evidence will bother some people. It bothers me. But again—these weapons are out there, and I believe they are being utilized.

First, I never heard any voices—ever. I don't mean to suggest that actual voices are not used on others, but I have heard nothing that sounded like an actual word.

As far as mind reading, Paul Baird offers a fair analysis of how it works, and how far—and how rapidly—it has progressed, using satellites and computers. But I have trouble believing mind reading can be done accurately.

Then, why am I suspecting electronic assault if I'm not hearing voices or believing that my mind is being read? Well, there are likely a host of other things going on. Sound is a complex phenomenon. Different wave lengths do different things to different minds. Combining these wave lengths may do even more. I have heard, since 2001, a cacophony of deep bass, baritone, and even tenor-like noises. Nothing like high pitched tinnitus. These deep droning sounds are relentless, undulating, and sleep and concentration inhibitors.

The sounds were in my home and yard, not at others'

homes that I would visit for many days. Early one May morning, I couldn't sleep because of it, and at daybreak I hiked about a mile to a railroad track to see if a diesel engine might be idling. Nothing in either direction.

A year later, I found someone else who heard the same kind of noise. Someone on the same wavelength, no doubt.

I mention the noise phenomenon for several reasons. The Patriot Act was enacted. Then, the noises began. Then, my demeanor changed. Nothing too overt or anything that I couldn't control, but change I did. I thought I was suffering from the cynicism of age. I still cannot be perfectly certain.

I have mentioned how my very language changed. I would catch myself repeating, sometimes aloud, a word or phrase that I would never have said before the sounds began. Could these have been imbedded, subliminally, in the sounds. Or could certain combinations of wavelengths create words in one's mind. Some of the literature says they can.

When we take a new medicine, we are encouraged to look at the possible side-effects and to discontinue use if we suspect that the medicine is harmful. If there are seven or eight potential side-effects listed, and we experience each and every one, we would likely conclude that the relationship factor is undeniable.

Using "side-effects" of electronic assault as mentioned from just the Jim Keith and Paul Baird sources, I have come up with a short list of just eight items. I have experienced at least seven. They are:

(1) Continual droning sounds at my residences.

(2) Violent, horrible nightmares—mostly in the last seven or eight years, but nothing similar in any way prior. (My wife, during the worst periods, has opted to sleep in another room. I don't blame her at all.)

(3) Very loud, explosive popping in the back of the head.

(4) Severe heart palpitations.

(5) Sharp stinging sensations, on nerve endings, not like chigger bites, but almost as painful.

(6) Blurred vision (caused by lasers).

(7) Alteration of brain chemistry and emotional state, caused by HAARP microwaves (brain chemistry I can hardly prove, but a shift in emotional state is all too obvious.)

(8) Hearing voices—not really. But I am reminded of driving along, or just sitting and finding myself repeating a word or short phrase THAT WAS NOT MINE!

Add to these "side-effects" the eczema, the incessant helicopters, the harassment, and the **history** of the agencies, I conclude that I am likely being assaulted.

Indeed, Jim Keith, in his book Mass Control, states: ". . . during its history, the CIA has been *the* [my emphasis] prime player in formulating a secret science of mind control . . . ."

December 6, 2013

As I continue this writing on December 6, 2013, I will mention that today, several miles from home, a helicopter tailed me for about a mile or so down the four lane highway, then veered in the direction of my house.

Yesterday, slightly rainy, I came out from a hospital visit to the parking lot and saw beside the car what looked like a gallon of gas that had leaked onto the asphalt. My mind did no connection until my eye noticed the cigarette butt lying in the middle of the rainbow colors. Could it be . . . ? You're never certain about anything. These are masters of chaos, confusion, propaganda, torment, murder, thievery, and starting wars that kill millions of innocents.

Truly, it would not take a devious mastermind to conclude that one Dr. Corkin Cherubini, whistleblower, civil rights advocate, peace advocate, CIA critic, currently finishing two books (with much of the profit going toward civil rights and liberties work), aging and slightly eccentric, and no "little angel," would be the world's best target to label as a terrorist—even if the government agency in charge of this deviousness has to go to great lengths to set up and frame him. These agencies are the world's most devious, and with unlimited resources, can create fear, pain, and civil strife around the world.

The irony—for them—is ideal: if you're white and try to correct societal wrongs against minorities, you will be tortured and/or dead. Ditto for any people of color. And what is unearthly and frightening is that a miniscule percentage can kill all they desire. Only a few of their forces may die while millions of American citizens perish. Look at the Iraq war figures. (My mother watches hours of FOX "news" each day, and she was persuaded that the Trayvon decision would start a race war, and we could all end up dead. I told her repeatedly that could never happen. I also stated to her that it could be the scenario the government wanted—an excuse to unleash the killing power on innocent people. NSA, CIA, H.S., etc., all have my comments recorded. The public will never hear the 99.99% "they" don't want you to hear.

December 8, 2013

This is day ninety-nine after August 30, and a day I have been dreading. My head has been feeling as if it is compressing painfully. Unlike any headache in my life. I am also very disoriented—almost like being half awake and sick at the same time. I kept reading accounts of the people the CIA had experimented on, and wondered if it was contrived. If not, why had I not had any of this harsher electronic or microwave torture? (And/or chemicals/drugs?) The night before last "compression" began, and when I awoke this morning, the feeling was one of an invisible force pushing inward all around the top of the head. I read accounts with a skeptical eye, even as I suspected what I was up against, so if you, the reader, are feeling doubt, that doubt is healthy and wise. At the same time, I plead that you research on your own more about CIA mind control and also the use of ELF and microwave weaponry, as well as CIA DRUG experiments. Chances are that these weapons are not just for use on some real, or contrived, enemies of the state. They are being used on *us*—now!

March 8, 2014

Eighty-four days, twelve unbelievable weeks, since my "final" last entry.

I have spent scores of hours on the internet researching the topics of microwave mind control/torture/murder and gang stalking (predatory and governmental). The learning curve has been something similar to that of a child who has not yet started school, suddenly entering the best progressive Waldorf type kindergarten.

It would be nice if this could be my final entry and draw nice closure with a pleasant ending, but from all I hear, there is rarely an end to being a "targeted individual."

Targeted Individual, or TI, is the name for those of us chosen for torture by the government, or even an independent group, gang, or organization—generally called *gang stalkers*, and not to be confused with street hoodlum gangs.

The "gangs" we have seen are primarily municipal vehicles (legions of sheriff cars, fire trucks, and all types of emergency vehicles . . . more in a week than one would expect to see in a year). These vehicles abound as we travel the roads or streets. Also, what appears to be coerced or paid "citizens" follow in the stores or on the sidewalks, often using noisemakers, yelling, or talking unusually loudly. These actions are just the "nuisance" aspect, although seeing what seems like all (it's not all!) of law enforcement under the thumbs of controllers is demoralizing.

Once I started using the internet again, it was a matter of less than thirty minutes of searching before I realized that I was experiencing what is usually termed *Gang Stalking* or *Organized Stalking*. The web had hundreds of accounts of this phenomenon. "You Tube" also has great information and help, although, like all internet material, there will be the bogus items to distract the unwary. One of my family members admitted to thinking gang stalking/microwave mind control was possibly a hoax after just a few minutes of reading, but after going further, saw that it is no doubt as real as real can be, even though it sounds like science fiction to someone who has not experienced it.

I recalled my own reaction to an article on the topic about two years prior: it seems really horrible, *if indeed it's really true*, but why worry too much. IT COULD NEVER HAPPEN TO ME!

Yet, it had been happening. For years! The 24/7 surveillance of every room and every vehicle will likely begin years before you know of it. This is what covert agencies do

> "It appears that those who administer the program (Gang Stalking) can call any location in the U.S. for surveillance, a telephone tap, or . . . harassment directed at a victim, and immediately dispense manpower to the source. This well-greased covert operation makes the old FBI COINTELPRO look like a Sunday School class."
> —Ted Gunderson
> Former FBI Chief,

best—spy. For decades if needed.

The microwave mind control (and possibly drugs and chemicals, as well) will commence long before you realize it is happening. One does not have to hear voices! One technology apparently uses "skull to brain" messaging, causing the victim to clearly hear easily recognizable words and phrases, often delivered with sound effects to give the impression of "a voice of god" or "a voice of the devil."

I was puzzled for much of the past six months (the length of time for this diary and my lack of knowledge of the well-orchestrated harassment program) as to why I had **all** the major symptoms of microwave mind control/torture/murder, and yet I hadn't heard the "voices" that experts in the field like Paul Baird kept mentioning.

Then, just a few weeks ago, I read someone's description of the "voice" she had heard as being something like a Darth Vader voice. That night I listened for Darth—and there it was! Barely. Almost totally subliminal. I strained to understand the words, but they were lost in a synthetic distance. It was that same synthetic sound I had heard thousands (or millions) of times before.

Just last night I listened to Michael F. Bell talk on "Coast to Coast" about his life as a TI, and his not hearing recognizable "human voices" experience was like my own. Incidentally, the two hour interview with writer Michael Bell and investigator Roger Tulces is one of the more comprehensive and enlightening (and truly frightening) information pieces I have come across. Ironically, the person who recommended this "Coast to

Coast" program was a New Hampshire police officer. Again, *not all* the police are totally under control of whatever government force is directing this Nazi Gestapo scenario. It is painful for us to see so many state and municipal employees utilized in a government gang stalking program. Would I do it? Probably. If my family's existence depended upon it. My heart goes out not only to the victims of gang stalking, but also to many of the perpetrators who have little or no choice.

At least I knew, early on, just **why** I had been targeted: my work in education led to some astounding discoveries about racial hard tracking in my own school system. I tried to correct it, and there was quite an adverse reaction, to put it mildly. A media spotlight on the situation helped immensely—but did, of course, include some of the problems accompanying media coverage. Overall, though, I thought the major media did an excellent job of informing the public of inequities that could be found in many public schools, not just mine.

While I never thought of what I did as "whistleblowing," a number of visitors and writers did mention the word. And today (actually, almost six months ago), we are informed that there is a "**War on Whistleblowers.**" There is even an award winning documentary film that is so entitled.

Not one single person I have talked with has any negative feeling about the service of Edward Snowden and many others who have exposed problems in government. Yet, we see nonstop efforts to ruin the lives of our current field of whistleblowers. These efforts are nothing new. Let's go back a couple of decades:

"Let's nail Dr. Corkin Cherubini. This man was treated as a hero when we should have taught him a lesson." I can almost "hear the voices.

Paul Baird says that even before the "Patriot Act," there were laws stating that involuntary experimentation could be carried out on whistleblowers and dissenters. And I had even "dissented" a bit on matters of war and peace and such since my days as a whistleblower. So what should I expect?! Actually, I expected anything but harassment and inhumane torture.

Speaking of inhumane torture, I would like to mention, mostly in simplified lay terms, what I have learned over the past few weeks about microwave mind control/torture/murder.

It is called, by some, **non-lethal**. Yet, it will cause cancer, leukemia, tumors, heart failure, and/or a host of other problems. Thus, its effects can be extremely lethal. This directed energy can be as lethal as a bullet or a bomb. But it seems to be a new "darling" on the killing fields since it hardly leaves a trace. No bullet holes and no shrapnel. Just another cancer or heart attack victim.

Of course, a Hitlerian mind would see much more potential for directed microwave energy weaponry: it can be used for mind and behavior control with astonishing success—under *any* conditions.

Microwaves are radio frequency waves. Early experimenters discovered quickly that particular frequencies could elicit certain emotional responses in humans—an entire range from joy to anger to depression. Charts show which frequencies cause which feelings.

Then, there are combinations of frequencies. What if two or three or four are used in unison? Or pulsed? The possibilities are unlimited.

The same radio frequencies can be used for voice (or synthetic voice) to be broadcast to a victim. You hear a command and you believe it is from *your* own mind. You have always believed in your own better judgment. If the command is silly, you ignore it. But if it is repeated hundreds or thousands of times, can you continue to ignore it? It's difficult. Possibly impossible if you don't realize you are being programmed. As soon as you learn what is happening, it is much easier to fight.

For this reason, I believe the agencies or shadow government, or whoever, does not want this field of weaponry publicized or widely known about. They have done an **excellent** job of keeping it quiet. See how many major media articles you find on the topic of microwave mind control. If you find a few, do they **seriously** address this horrible issue or do they gloss over it?

Few articles attest, as Dr. Rauni Kilde, and I do, that: *"Microwave mind control is the biggest threat to humanity and the most sinister plan to enslave the human race forever."* (from "Microwave Mind Control: Modern Torture and Control Mechanisms Eliminating Human Rights and Privacy.")

If "they" cannot achieve their goal with microwaves and organized stalking, there is the **microchip**. Make it plural, Michael Bell tells us. Just think of the possibilities of a few dozen microchips nudging us in whatever direction the ultra controllers desire.

*"But our neat cell phones and big, cheap color TV's.
make up for microwaves and chips, don't they?"*

Two hours ago I was ready to add about a hundred
more pages. Now, I am deciding to do so would be
superfluous, especially since Michael F. Bell has two
hours on "Coast to Coast," as well as a book on his gang
stalking/microwave experience. My wife and I listened
critically for two hours last night and found almost
everything to be precisely in line with what we had
experienced. We were not abducted and heavily
drugged, but I have experienced maser (or pulsed
microwave) assault. I would also presume that we have
had heavier municipal vehicle escort than Michael.

Lately, our microwave assault appears to have
diminished greatly, upon the arrival of a Trifield
microwave oven leak detector. "They" know every move
we make, and we assumed that the day we took delivery
of the meter, the microwaving would halt. It has, so far.

Solid information from Dr. Rauni Kilde, Paul Baird,
and the late Jim Keith, in his book <u>Mind</u> <u>Control</u>, <u>Mass</u>
<u>Control</u>, clearly illustrates that the technology (and evil
intent) was largely here a decade and a half ago.

In fact, I encourage the public to read everything "out
there" on this set of issues, and understand that there will
be the bogus sites and comments. "They" will want to
protect their power.

Still, the more you know about it, the better off you,
your family, your friends, and your country will be.
Never make the mistake I made and say, *"It can never
happen to me!"*

March 12, 2014

Yet Another Dispiriting Note

I just watched Jesse Ventura's forty-three minute investigative documentary on microwave mind control—again. It's worth viewing. Twice!

Get to the end where former CIA veteran, Mark Phillips, tells us that it is the **mainstream** government that is doing the evil—not a rogue element.

The final interview with Harvard/MIT graduate, Dr. Robert Duncan, who went to work for the CIA and helped create the microwave mind control technology, says citizens are not just being harassed by microwaves, but tortured as well. He next says "they" want to control us from conscious to unconscious. And when Jesse Ventura asks him if it is too late to do anything about it and if *every* American will be controlled, Dr. Duncan replies, "I actually believe it is too late."

Many of us are not going to be able to accept Dr. Duncan's bleak forecast. I admit that I am one, and I will, like Jesse Ventura and many others, be glad to give my last breath to insure *freedom of the mind*.

March 16, 2014

An excellent You Tube video by a **Targeted Individual** told us to stand firm and think positively about the situation we are in. Don't give in! Play it down to the wire!

I felt stronger after a verbal stimulus. Then, the TI said to think of the situation as "a chess game." An interesting analogy, and certainly appropriate at times.

But later, I thought of an improved analogy: you take your seat at the prepared chess table and notice your side of the board has *one* piece—a pawn!

Your opponent, you notice, has two castles and twenty-four queens! And this opponent just happens to be the World Champion for the last seven years.

The plight of the TI: one small individual with very limited resources vs. one thousand "experts" in every criminal field—with billions of Black Operations dollars and unlimited resources.

March 20, 2014

The Unbelievable 200 Day Update

A milestone for a major target, I feel certain. It is Thursday, a few days after St. Patrick's Day, and I feel fairly lucky to be alive. "Fairly" because of the everyday conditions—**but** we have come to grips with extinction and the torture.

Even so, last night was the closest brush I've had so far, including the directed energy (pulse beam, maser type) attack on me over a month ago. Just twelve hours ago, while I was sitting, petting my dog, relaxed, thinking of nothing except being with my dog—my heart just seemed to <u>quit</u>. My breath stopped for quite a few seconds. I couldn't move. I couldn't breathe. A natural impulse made me force coughing, over and over, just to get air, and, I suppose, to get the heart going again.

In a minute, still having to cough/breathe, I was in the den with my wife, trying to tell her what was happening. She was petrified. In a few minutes, I was almost back to normal, however, but with a cough/breath necessary from time to time. Plenty of chest pain for the next two hours.

I checked an internet site that addressed induced heart attacks, and the comment was—it takes "them" about one second to induce the heart attack—one punch of a button. For seventy years, my heart has been perfect, except for the past few months when **induced** palpitations occurred. The point I want to stress is that *any* heart problem (attack or total stoppage) will be the result of "their" directed energy attacks.

They have any number of murder methods, I know, and hundreds of thousands of perpetrators vying to carry them out for even a small reward.

Why the drastic measure yesterday? We had called or emailed dozens of media, political offices (including those of the Senate Intelligence Oversight Committee), and even individuals about the insanity of government condoned/supported gang stalking. Later, we wondered about the *extent* of CIA spying on Senate Intelligence Committee members and their staffs, and whether even they were being gang stalked.

I could prolong my life, I feel, by quietly accepting whatever tortures "they" feel like subjecting us to, but I just can't do that. Maybe there's a genetic thing inside that says "You must warn the other innocent people." That's fine with me. One life to save thousands—or millions—is mathematically and humanely sound.

In the past few weeks, I have had four directed energy attacks (one very serious), and my wife had one that could have been serious since she crumpled to hard pavement. We have her fall on the driveway security recording. She also got a picture of a recent helicopter cruising not far from the house. Most things are "unprovable," the way one would expect covert agencies to operate.

Still, even if we had irrefutable evidence—to whom would we take it? The more I read, the greater the complicity seems to be, including professionals of every type. Then, too, if the agencies and their perps can turn all friends and family into enemies, what can you expect from, say . . . an attorney or a municipal worker.

When victims have such a total lack of support, it is easy to understand how an entire population of whistle blowers, dissenters, activists, or simply anyone who questions the wrong power figure could become extinct. It doesn't matter that whistle blowers and activists work hard for a better country and world—often risking their own welfare. The perpetrators and community members are told *lies* about these **targeted individuals,** or TI's, portraying them as perverts or hard core criminals of some sort. Never in my seventy years have I been any of these deviant persons, and there is little chance of becoming one after seventy. Still, during my last two years in political office in '95-'96, there was a never ceasing campaign to label me as a homosexual. Not true; but in that rural area in 1995, even the hint that one's sexual orientation differed from their norm was often reason for persecution and unfair treatment. Even today, such attitudes exist and not just in rural settings. Another civil rights/humanitarian issue that is far from resolved.

Some of these agencies have had decades (over half a century!) in perfecting slander, character defamation, LSD experimentation, mind control, prostitution and pedophile rings, heroin trafficking, political assassination, and almost any other atrocious act known to man. They have made both a science and art form of the most evil and inhumane torturous acts any imagination could devise. I, for one, have no difficulty believing that we have government agencies and departments that would have huge buildings full of American citizens decimated in order to start a war or further a political agenda.

Yet, some still defer to these groups. Not only

defer—but grovel, making certain they have all the billions and trillions of dollars they could ever conceivably use for any devious purpose—with *no* Congressional oversight! *No* rules! *No* limits. *No* boundaries for anything! (Well, maybe . . . if they are spying on the **wrong** senator . . . .)

It is the opinion of this writer, in the event the reader has not already consciously deduced as much, that many of our agencies do *not* need ridiculously ineffective Congressional oversight. These agencies need total dissolution!

"Every breath I take—air mixed with chemicals, drugs, and or poison—reminds me that millions of Americans are deliberately being MURDERED by their own government."

—Dr. Corkin Cherubini

April 2, 2014

An incredible 216 days since I began. Plenty of action since my last entry. Not much time to write.

The huge red spots on my legs keep getting larger, and one is turning black. I went to a doctor yesterday, but he couldn't see me without an appointment, and that gives the perps time to flood in. So I went to the nearby hospital, a smaller facility but one with an excellent staff. They did blood testing and several other tests in half the time it took the doctor at the New England hospital to *glance* at my legs and say "eczema." But fifteen or twenty minutes after my arrival at the New England hospital emergency facility, the perps began filing into the waiting room, and strangely, many of them were seen before I was.

Yesterday, the doctor thought I might have some type of systemic fungus. She also said it did not appear to be cancerous. Great news!

Still, I get the feeling that the "fungus" (if that's what it is) came from the chemicals that are permeating the house and garage. More importantly, I would think it is some biochemical concoction that is experimental, and who knows what will happen.

Day to day, for the last few weeks, has centered around keeping us (and our pets) away from the worst of the fumes. I wrote letters to SPCA and PETA last night, telling them that I have seen far too many articles (and some pictures) of gang stalking victims' pets suffering, along with their humans, from torturous drugs, chemicals, and microwave directed energy. It would be ironic (but wonderful) if the animal action groups were the ones to initiate an action plan against gang stalking torture and murder. Certainly, it doesn't appear that the media or humanitarian groups will take steps to stop the murder.

The chemicals/drugs flooding into the house ***must*** be controlled remotely. If we are in the kitchen, two or three minutes later, the smell will be there. My eyes and nasal passages will burn with the fresh release. The same pattern is repeated in whatever rooms we retreat to so we go outdoors. After five or ten minutes of fresh air, we brave the chemicals again. We must write more letters, make more calls about this assault. We are feeling more certain that time is running out. I get the urge to tell the editors—**YOU MAY NOT HAVE ANOTHER CHANCE TO HEAR US!**

Many of the targets are doctors. Dr. John Hall, Dr. Rauni Leena Kilde, Dr. Robert Duncan—just to mention several. My wife and I thought being doctors would give more credibility to our situation, but it has not so far. Most people we talk with listen politely, but rather than ask any pertinent questions, they seem to be wondering if all this "torture and murder" can be taken seriously. We can tell what they're thinking; we've dealt with hundreds of humans daily in our careers. So, we end up by saying, "We understand that what we are telling you may sound preposterous—like so much science fiction—so please, if you can, look at some of the internet and You Tube sites on **Gang Stalking.** I'm betting most do ***not*** research it. I recall one writer beginning his piece by saying, "If you're not a TI (targeted individual), do ***not*** read this article. You will not be able to really comprehend or believe much of what I am saying."

> *"Every day for the mind control victims, it's like the rape victim who has to go out and interact in the society where her rapist is still at large. The difference is that there is a whole conspiracy of rapists and they rape the victims each and every day.*
> —*Allen L. Barker*

The writer continued to elaborate on current mind control technology and where it will be shortly: to a point that your every thought can be read, your mind continuously raped. I cannot find the actual article again on the internet, but I wish I could give credit.

One of my underlying themes has been that you don't have to be a major whistleblower, an activist, or a creative writer to get targeted. I have found too many cases where the victim has no idea about why he/she is being harassed and tortured. And, as the crop of whistleblowers and dissenters becomes totally extinct, even more people will be asking, "Why Me?" It won't be because they are prostitutes, pimps, pedophiles, perverts, terrorists, racists, or criminals, as the gang stalkers accuse them of being.

I am 180° opposite of any of the lies which I am certain "they" have used. For two years in 1995 and 1996, "they" used the homosexual theme, a "90's" hot button that assures "them" of public support in some locales. (Like racism, gay bashing has *not* disappeared!) Imagine if they told the public, "He's a whistleblower who was making education fairer in America."

The lies "they" smear will spread constantly to the point that you may begin to doubt your *own* integrity and sanity. Researcher Paul Baird reminds us all firmly: *"You are not insane; they are the villains.* They are the ones who will even commit serious crimes so they can blame you."

And we must never forget that "they" have an arsenal of drugs, chemicals, and psychotropic weaponry that can make anyone *say* or even *do* anything "they" want the victim to do so "their" accusations will seem true. Avoiding the traps is easier if you know what is being done to you. They don't want you to know—thus the media/societal blackout on gang stalking and the very lethal, murderous, torturous weaponry used.

You Tube has a fair share of excellent commentary and personal experiences concerning gang stalking. A great one I viewed just a couple of evenings ago was a monologue by a woman who encouraged TI's to remain positive and hopeful and to never give up. She compared the struggle to a chess game. Yes, except sometimes you know it's like coming to sit down at the board, and you see your opponent's side with twenty-four queens and two castles. You have one pawn on your side. Then, your opponent walks in, and he is a seven time world champion. But even with the "slightly" uneven playing field, you still have a few options . . . .

So, now, after 216 days of knowing for certain that "they" were out to get me—thousands of them—who is to blame? After hundreds of hours researching gang stalking, hundreds more lying awake nights trying to piece it all together; after thousands of hours dealing with the perpetrators and the plumbers, electricians, HVAC, and natural gas service people or shielding against EMF's or trying to dodge chemical/drug vapors; after days of excruciating stomach and leg pains that started *after* the hovering helicopters, to the isolation and psychological damage that comes from active hatred, or the brain damage that comes from microwave and drug/chemical assault, you realize that your opponents are powerful enough to control every human on the planet, not just during their waking hours, but also during their sleep. The controllers almost have the technology for *mass control* in place NOW! (While I was saying, "Not me! My mind's too tough!" they were controlling my thoughts at that very moment. Whether it's an LSD witches' brew or a simple microwave cooking   your brain   cells   or   subliminal impressions repeated—repeated thousands of times, day and night, they *will* have control.)

I would almost like to simplify, blame myself, talk to a few psychologists, and let it go at that. I mean, can 10,000 perpetrators all be wrong—even if they are parolees, released mental hospital patients, those in dire need, those under the thumb of a powerful agency boss, or a murderous sadist. But Paul Baird reminds us firmly, *we* are not crazy. They are the ones engaged in first degree, cold-blooded murder and committing crimes to set up and frame innocent people. And I firmly agree with Mr. Baird.

Realizing that each case may be slightly different (but with an uncanny structural similarity), I am still speaking from my own personal reference parameters.

The first indicator that was concrete and tangible was the helicopters hovering over the house, circling my three acre lot, and doing slow cruise overs. (Again, in nine years of continual and extensive driving around this area, I have never seen one of the large Chinook unmarked black helicopters.) Would the helicopter pilot share in the blame? I would think not. If his orders came from a military/agency, he'd best follow them. But the person who ordered the aerial surveillance? YES! Emphatically. Will we ever find that person? My wife and I made visits to two local law enforcement departments, and they were truly as much in the dark as we were. The local FBI would not answer or return our many calls, but we did get a large city agent about sixty miles away, and he suggested calling the nearby Air Force base. We did, but they said they had no helicopters, but that an Air Force National Guard unit on the base might. We called them, but again received no satisfactory answer. Still, the fact is *someone* ordered those huge unmarked black helicopters to hover over and repeatedly circle our home.

The next very scary and noticeable assault to the psyche was the unusually heavy police and emergency vehicle presence occurring a day after I mentioned, in the "privacy" of my kitchen that I would sue a government agency for $1.2 billion dollars. (This presence persists to this very day almost everywhere I go.) Are the police or emergency vehicle drivers to blame? For the most part, probably *not*. I have been "caught in the middle" of situations myself and followed what was possibly a poor directive. These police cruisers and emergency vehicle drivers were following someone's directive. Blaming them would make as much sense as blaming a perpetrator on parole who knew what he'd better do if he were to stay out of jail.

There are much higher places to lay blame. I have accused the media, I know, for not informing the other ninety-nine percent of the population that has never heard of gang stalking, much less the murderous nature of a program straight from Nazi and Stasi Germany! When I talk to reporters, though, it takes only a few minutes to realize that these folks are not going into shark infested waters. No boat rocking there.

I can't blame the reporter/editor for avoiding a hot topic. After all, staying alive and healthy is more important than getting a Pulitzer Prize. But I do blame the *corporate controllers* of our sick media. A media that seems obsessed with obfuscation, instead of saving possibly millions of innocent American lives.

Politicians share in the blame, to be sure, but I

honestly wonder if the bulk of our state, local, and national politicians know any more about the *gang stalking* program than I did just seven months ago. Until two months ago, I had heard the term briefly—only once. Media again!? Yes. Partially. But the biggest player—along with the corporate controllers—is sitting right there in Washington, D. C. The Pentagon.

I imagine there is very little agreement about *when* America became a military-police state, but from what most of my own research says, we have been there for quite a while, and we are seeing it become more entrenched day by day. And our country is not the only victim of this unchecked military-police state power. The controllers have sufficient power to decimate any society anywhere. Decimate? No, eradicate!

The gang stalking phenomenon has shown that politics by and for a military-police state is not just inhumane, but insane. Bills and directives giving the military the right to experiment or torture/harass/murder citizens who might protest or disagree with the controllers' agenda are just as bad as what predominated in Nazi/Stasi Germany.

Then, too, I think of *where* the equipment (helicopters, masers, active denial weapons, HAARP and GWEN towers, warfare chemicals and drugs, etc.) and the training to use this equipment are coming from. The source is certainly *not* civilian fare.

Finally, the intelligence agencies must be recognized as nothing more than a military adjunct—all connected:

CIA, NSA, DHS, as well as those of which most of us are unaware. I have mentioned that much of the military/agency activity and expenditure is classified or secret at a time when we need ever greater transparency and congressional oversight. To this end, a quote from "The Silent Massacre" by Max Williams is appropriate:

"The human resources and the enormous cost required to carry out electronic stalking and mind control, reinforced in many cases by organized stalking, almost certainly limits its use to governments.

Only governments can mobilize the enormous outlay of funds and successfully camouflage the use of those funds. Only governments have sophisticated highly classified equipment and computers required for electronic abuse and mind control. Only governments can train in secrecy the cadre of handlers who administer the electronic assault and mind control activities, using deception and psychology. The intelligence community in the U.S. operates with an almost limitless secret budget without Congressional oversight."

Nicholas Kirkland also warns of "disinformation sites" that steer readers away from the truth.

From the first flights and hoverings of large, black Chinook helicopters, to the sophisticated electronic assault directed at us, to the exotic drug/chemical deliveries in our vehicles and home—*everything* points to a massive government operation. I tend to think back to 1995-1996 each day—comparing what is happening to us now with the things that happened then. Far too similar for coincidence. The smear campaigns (homosexual; reverse discriminator). The propaganda machines. The isolation. The property and vehicle damage. The less organized, but very much present perpetrators. The attempt to burn our home down. The never ending threats. The use of chemicals and bio-weaponry (though miniscule compared with their use today). And the surveillance, though low tech by today's standards, the bevy of watchers and the phone taps.

From the earliest entries in my diary, there was constantly the thought that today was directly related to my blowing the whistle a full two decades earlier. Why wait for two decades!? To give a recuperation period? A respite? Or maybe my moves were hard to keep up with. No. Absolutely not. They never really stopped.

But, how do I know that they realized, after a mountain of highly positive media coverage, that it would be best to wait a while. Let it all fade out of memory while they employ their extreme surveillance, their mind control electronics, their drugs, chemicals, and continuous smear campaigns, always using the psychology gleaned from the Nazi-Stasi-KKK, MK ULTRA, COINTELPRO campaigns. With the very latest technology. And with the hearty consent of our lawmakers and media silence on a torturous/murderous program that is affecting millions of citizens.

But each day I kept asking myself—always knowing the answer before I asked: Why not sooner? Why so much expense and expenditure of manpower? Why years of costly mind control? (All those years I didn't even know for certain what sinister forces were working on me.) Why twenty years of surveillance instead of a few weeks or a few months? Is it *that* hard to get the exact words that "they" want? (Remember I *gave* them my *worst* as I was contemptuously defiant of any invasion of my privacy. I suspected then but gave them the filth that I thought peeping Toms and spies deserved.) And as I was giving them what I thought they deserved, they were stockpiling.

Stockpiling? You ask, "Why would *anyone* want to go to this effort for *you*?"

The perpetrators don't know why they have been told to do what they do, and they don't really want to hear an hour of history in one minute. But I know, and I have known all along. It will possibly be the link into more writings. I don't want to elaborate now, but I will suggest reading:

James Douglass, JFK and the Unspeakable
Amy and David Goodman, Static
Jim Mars, All his works

Possibly a glance at the indexes will be sufficient.

Perhaps just looking under three letters in the index of each: CIA. Under those three letters, don't spend too much time on those items about which we already know quite a bit, like complicity in heroin trafficking, or smear campaigns, or torture, or disinformation, or kidnapping. All horribly dark, evil endeavors. But the darker ones you can readily find. Such evil weighs a nation down like a man with one hundred albatrosses around his neck.

Our entire nation knows of this dark evil, and knows that the evil still exists and persists—MORE HORRIDLY than ever. It is an oppressive weight that grows each day because the EVIL force has not been stopped. Instead, it has multiplied many times, and has grown ever more hideous. (One powerful agency can, and will, subvert the best intentions of *all* our municipal departments. I have seen this first hand.)

There is that connection between the darkest of their deeds—and me. They walked away in 1963 with only a few side glances. There was plenty of insulation and political protection—as there is today, of course. But with very brave people like Douglass and Mars (not to mention a few hundred other brave researchers) informing us, the *truth* will be known, and it will be followed with appropriate action.

This writer sees the necessity of the dissolution of agencies that have a worse than Orwellian record of delving into drug, chemical, and electronic mind control. Or into smear campaigns, or complicity in heroin trafficking, or torture, or assassination.

April 19, 2014

Yesterday was typical, at least in the sense of our attempts to survive. Most of the night was spent outside in lawn chairs, moving from the two in back to the lawn chairs in front of the house. The remote release mechanisms pick up your location—room to room and even outside, and waft the chemical into that area.

But, two nights ago was one of the scariest moments of my life. I dozed off at about 10:30 p.m. in the rear carport lawn chair, actually, next to the house with our van in front, blocking the view of the back yard and woods (not ours) beyond the yard.

An ambient light seemed slightly brighter, so I got up, still sleepy, and looked around. The moon was almost full, so that maybe explained the ambient brightness, but then I noticed from within the woods, a pinpoint of light that seemed to be moving. I watched, unmoving, from behind the van, glad that my cap and jacket were dark colors.

Slowly, the light moved in my direction. As it closed the gap by about half, I could see that a dozen or so small white lights were in a keyhole shape and above those were small, blinking red lights in a circle. The device looked about the size of a standup vacuum, but my contact lenses were out and I could not see the details too well.

My first thought froze me into breathless silence. Possibly I was seeing some type of directed energy weapon—maser, microwave pulse machine, or whatever. Having been hit four times by such energy, I was wondering if a van would offer much protection from the beams. A house did not.

For several minutes I was thinking, this really could

be the terrible end to a horrible nightmare. I remember wishing my wife were there. She was in bed, the chemicals still not even noticeable to her olfactory sense.

The light stopped moving toward me at about a hundred feet away, right at the tractor road that runs behind our house and yard. As I watched, still frozen, the small lights blinking, I thought of psyops. Maybe I was *hoping* I was just experiencing a psyoptic event. A big blinky light toy to put one on edge. My rationale for that was "they" seemed to know our every move. Wouldn't "they" know I was under the carport? But, if someone were doing *dirty work* for a *covert* group, wouldn't they be a little less *overt*?

Whoever was out there moved the device around for about thirty minutes. I felt the need to urinate, but I wasn't about to move. The bottom area of the light machine, I noticed, had what appeared to be five or six black tubes coming out of it. It looked a bit like an engine manifold.

Then, I heard voices. They were barely audible so there was nothing I could understand, but I could tell there were a least two voices.

My eyes stayed on the device until I heard a machine, further down the tractor road—maybe a hundred yards. The sound was more like a large fan than an engine. It whirled for a minute or so, and then there was the sound of a million BB's hitting the trees and leaves on the ground.

I moved a few feet, almost ready to go see what they were spraying into my woods, as well as someone else's. Common sense stopped me. I remembered how totally blinded, incapacitated, chest wrenching the directed energy blasts had been. I could investigate later.

Minutes later, the red and white light device was moving away, and the sprayer was sounding like a tropical deluge. I crouched and went into the house. I fell into bed with most of my clothes on and whispered to my wife about what I had seen. Her only question was, "Are you certain you weren't seeing lightening bugs?" It was after midnight and I went to sleep amidst the pungent chemical odor.

The next day, I dug twenty-five or so holes across from the area where the device had concentrated, wondering if tubing could be bringing in toxic chemicals to the house and yard. Plenty of roots, but no tubes. I also crawled

*"I keep thinking of the economics of government spy experimentation. Dollars mean nothing, it seems. Ironically, for a couple hundred thousand, they could sign up most **any** out of work, out of a bad marriage guy—for life! Instead, they spend hundreds of millions on one nonconsensual guy like me?!"*
—Dr. "C"

under the house for about an hour, looking for suspicious tubing or piping. I saw nothing. And my home inspector had already indicated he would likely find nothing.

"They" are not called covert for nothing.

The chemical seems to have taken over my system: most of the day, the taste and smell of it are with me. An accompanying wooziness, like vertigo, is often there. I recall reading somewhere that certain odors can drive some people, and some animals, to death. Maybe that is what they're testing on me. And much more.

I kept thinking back to the early diary pages and how much I had surmised, even before I had heard about group, gang, or organized stalking. All of these terms come nowhere near expressing the sheer horror of something many times worse than its COINTELPRO predecessor. Ex-FBI whistleblower, Ted Gunderson says that COINTELPRO is like a Sunday school picnic compared to today's gang stalking. No wonder it's called a *Silent Holocaust.*

While I was correct about many things early on, it has only been in the last few weeks that I have admitted being incorrect about when I became a Targeted Individual.

My wife has remained resolute on the *when*. "Earlier than that," she would say each time I mentioned a year. I could not admit that it could have been 1996 or even 1995! Twenty years ago?

What I had seen as a local problem was *not* just local. I saw angry locals every day and knew they *could* have done a lot of nasty deeds. Maybe.

I think the "when" is very important to TI's. It marks the end of a normal life for them. A goodly percentage of TI's mention the 90's, the 80's, or even the 70's as the year they became TI's.

For me, there were the never ending incidents and malicious criminal actions that seemed to end after I retired and left that area. But there was something wrong. Something hideously covert, it seemed. Not tangible, like slashed tires or threat calls or chemicals on door knobs or obvious perpetrator behavior at every turn. Something much more covert—what is referred to as "light targeting." Heavy surveillance and the beginning of isolation: the first two tactics of gang stalking.

Only after reading thousands of pages on gang stalking and thinking about "When did it really begin?" did I come to agree with my wife about 1995. Two decades—and eighteen or nineteen years of keeping it under wraps! The fortunes of taxpayer money to fund this devious activity. The wasted man hours to electronically mind control, to bug every location and then monitor, to pay perpetrators to make my life a little harder, to move armies of men and equipment wherever I go! I can't even believe it.

And for most of my life, I have led a fairly exemplary life as an educator and student. Until the year following retirement when the zaps and zings and stings and compression headaches began. The time when, along with surveillance and isolation, the mind melt begins.

Suddenly, *induced* dreams have me kicking and screaming and striking my wife as we both sleep. Often, several times a night I would scream until I was hoarse. The never ending multiple tones (not tinnitus) that most TI's have. In fact, I was experiencing most of the same "light targeting" occurrences that other TI's have described. But in September, 2013, the "light targeting" became more intense after I mentioned in the "privacy" of my own home that I would sue a government agency.

So, looking at a twenty year period for my destruction, I suppose we should all be very impressed! Twenty years of drugs and chemicals. Electronic mind control techniques. And all the personal and social sabotage that can be done by agencies with unlimited funding and a free rein.

I read where most all TI's marvel at the dollars invested to destroy them. I certainly do.

CIA, NSA, FBI, DHS, ETC., ETC., ETC., ETC., all know that *"We Are the Rats."* Not bad rats, but we are like the rats used in the extinction experiments of the 50's and 60's. These agencies know that we, like the rats, will become extinct in time without our private space and private thoughts.

Already, there is no private space—practically nowhere on earth that we can have a truly private conversation. They know where we are every second of the day with the many types of tracking and surveillance equipment they have. They have our thoughts. Most thoughts are obtainable now, and they can manipulate our emotions. From what researcher Paul Baird and others say, the entire mental cornucopia is near. Maybe it is even perfected as you read these words!

June 23, 2014

Last Notation: A Chilling Conclusion

Summer. Another milestone. This morning while Phyllis was gone to the market, my writing finished for awhile, I wandered around the house wondering if there was something constructive I should be doing. Nothing.

Except maybe clean up some of my clutter. The second RF meter (bug detector) we had bought lay on the table. I decided to use it to check my elbow (where a TI at the Philadelphia TI Conference a week before thought there might be a chip. He was checking everyone.) Also, I would check a hernia repair area from eleven years earlier. I remember that any type of surgery was ideal for microchip implanting. I had often thought about the "visiting" students who were observing the surgical procedure.

Nothing happened when I put the probe all around the elbow. On impulse, I stuck the probe into my mouth since I recalled how often chips are hidden in dental work. Again, nothing.

But as soon as the end of the antenna probe got near my hernia repair area, though, green and blue digital lights went off. (Blue lights indicate high intensity transmission; green lights, less intense, but still something to be very concerned about.) Again and again, right at the incision area, but nowhere else!

I lowered the sensitivity on the meter and just green lights came on. I tested other areas. Nothing. Back to the incision area. Green lights—over and over.

When Phyllis came back, we went through the process four more times, each time using one of four different video cameras. We have already heard of far too much evidence of any kind being stolen or being consumed in a mysterious fire (not so mysterious to "them" since "they" start them.)

All day, I had felt nauseous and lightheaded. By evening, it was worse. At 11:30 p.m., we drove fifteen miles to a rest stop to sleep because between 10:00 and 11:00 p.m., while I was asleep, the windshield and driver's window of the vehicle in which I was sleeping had large oily spots on them, and the chemical smell in the vehicle was overpowering. To me, not to my wife?!

I still felt sick as I contemplated the implications. I have not really delved into chips very much, but I had felt lucky because I thought I had at least escaped having a microchip.

Microwaves and direct energy weapons, poisons, and drugs, "accidents," and vandalism, untold hordes of perpetrators: your tax money used to kill you. Then, there is the microchip implant, put in place without either your permission or knowledge, and it is used to further guarantee *someone's* absolute, total control over everything you think, say, or do.

Some people won't care. They'll shrug and continue watching sitcom game shows or what they believe are "reality" shows. Others of us will feel that the game of life really is over. What's left but death and dying. Maybe. But if we still have a breath, we *can* fight back! The question is, will we?

The esteemed Dr. Rauni Kilde, from an internet article, tells us of the implications of the microchip:

"The mass media have not reported that an implanted person's privacy vanishes for the rest of his or her life. S/he can be manipulated in many ways. Using different frequencies, the secret controller of this equipment can even change a person's emotional life. S/he can be made aggressive or lethargic. Sexuality can be artificially influenced. Thought signals and subconscious thinking can be read, dreams affected, and even induced, all without the knowledge or consent of the implanted person . . . . Mind control can be used for political purposes. The goal of mind controllers today is to induce the targeted persons or groups to act against their own convictions or best interests."

June 24, 2014

I never thought of myself as a **Whistleblower** in the mid 90's, or did I know there was a war on Whistleblowers. Others did, however.

If our government had a "security" force comprised of drug lords, kingpin pedophile and prostitution pimps, legions of presidential, political, and general population assassins, and drug and electronic mind control technocrats doing Nazi-type experimentation, would the public support such an endeavor???

Ironically, we have had such a program for many decades, and the public and the politicos, for the most part, give them a free reign to do ANYTHING—and MORE MONEY THAN EVEN IMAGINABLE TO DO IT WITH!

Yes, "they" have told the media ("their" media) that it's for "security." We listen, we trust it, and we buy it. Thus, their *evil* permeates the very fabric of our nation.

June 25, 2014

As I zoomed into my 60's, I was astonished with a new found ability to say obnoxious things (most of which I did not mean or even believe!). Cynical, sexist, racist—all obnoxious.

In time, I led myself to believe I had "reached a new level of maturity." Yes, I had often heard that most older guys become cynical and sarcastic as they aged. Possibly I was "maturing" a few years earlier!

Still, I amazed myself. After one racist comment, I recall sitting dumbfounded, thinking, "Why is such a comment coming from me? After all, the African American community saved my neck, saved my sanity, repeatedly. Such words, or even thoughts, made no sense. I took comfort in the fact that those words in no way reflected my true feelings and attitude, but I was disturbed that this *strange* new level of maturity seemed to know no bounds.

At that point, 2003 to 2013, I had no inkling of microwave mind control or microchip *TOTAL* control. I had heard something of the horror of CIA LSD experimentation. Even in September of 2013, as I began thinking through reasons for my plight, I did not suspect chemical/drug or microwave assault as even a possibility. Much less a *microchip!!*

Yet, I knew that certain "forces" could, and would, in their years of 24/7 surveillance find quite a few instances of "uncharacteristic" language. AND USE THEM TO DISCREDIT ME, THUS UNDERMINING A LIFETIME OF POSITIVE WORKS!

I then believed—and still do—that the "forces" were a powerful citizenry combined with the ultra powerful agencies that have spent decades developing inhuman programs such as MK ULTRA and COINTELPRO.

These programs **still exist**, according to many insiders!

It has been only a few months since I realized that I have been microwaved **and** drugged/chemicalized for almost twenty years! And for only a few days, now, has what was just a nagging possibility turned into a nightmare reality: being microchipped, without my knowledge or permission, during surgery.

When human beings are totally mind controlled with a constant array of chemicals, drugs, microwaves, and horrid microchips, these humans are essentially dead—at least mind and soul dead.

I feel that a major part of me died in 1997-98, when the early signs of chemicals and microwaves were noticed, though not on a cognizant level.

By early 2014, after knowing more about "their" control methods, rejection of the control has become more possible. Of course, the chemical and microwave intensities have increased and pose serious health threats. I don't know, yet, how serious a factor the microchip might be, but for the while, at least, I will trust Dr. Rauni Kilde's analysis (see pages 123-124).

June 26, 2014

Drone Concerns

Drones are with us, I am loath to keep discovering. They are like small helicopters that can go anywhere. Or they may be like fairly large planes that can be armed with most anything.

At home in the South, we have seen several (and have photos), and while I was guarding (sleeping in) a "clean" car to keep the perpetrators from chemicalizing/toxifying it, I awakened to the whirring of what I took to be a drone. Within a minute, the chemical smell flooded the car and environs.

Yesterday, June 25, we got back to our cabin in rural Maine, expecting it to be freshly contaminated with chemicals. It was. The rugs. The curtains. All furniture. The bedding. We opened all windows and doors and turned on three large fans. It helped.

But at 3:00 a.m., I awoke with my nostrils burning and a dizziness that made getting out of bed difficult. By 3:05 a.m., I was outside, walking around the large drive and deck. Then, at 3:20 a.m. I looked up and saw lights—several moving lights. They were two or three times higher than the tallest of our trees. They leisurely (and silently) cruised over the house, drive, and barn, and then out of vision.

After the car spraying incident, I had checked the web for "spraying" drones. The first article was about how dirty Chinese drones were spraying chemtrails. Nothing about American drones.

But I doubt that a Chinese drone came half way around the world to spray *me*. Drones are probably as close as the nearest military base—or neighbor.

We may want to recheck "chemtrails." A few years ago, I scoffed, thinking it sounded like another scare tactic. Indeed, it is, and we need to be scared unless we don't mind seeing large, *selected* segments of our population poisoned to an early death. Like HAARP, chemtrails could easily decimate an entire continent in quick time. Type in C-H-E-M-T-R-A-I-L-S. Like Gang Stalking, it's blocked out of most media.

And, on July 28, 2014

I feel more positive by far than I did six or even twelve months ago. I'm not even sure *why*. Possibly because I've done everything I could do to disseminate what I now know, and I have discovered that hardly a soul seems to know about or even be able to comprehend what is happening to our citizens. We can still hardly believe it!

Having done what we can (educating many thousands by now about a maniacal program for mind control, torture, and murder in America), we can well leave the remainder to providence, fate . . . whatever. Of course, what we really have been able to do is microscopic compared to what "they" have done and will continue to do with their ungodly unlimited resources.

In less than a year, we have gone from near perfect health to what looks and feels like physical wrecks. We have watched as all that we have worked and planned for is thrown into question. We have watched as our very reputations have been masterfully destroyed by some of the world's most devious propaganda and smear agents. We have wasted a large segment of our senior years documenting bizarre stalking, documenting very strange "accidents" and occurrences, photographing everything from suspected perps to visiting helicopters and planes, to direct energy blasts, to too many chemtrails to mention, to late night microwave RF meter readings. We have visited many attorneys, law enforcement offices, political offices, as well as the media.

A year wasted? We cannot see it like that. What we see is our utmost attempt to tell America that most (99%) of them could very soon be in the same boat as we are now. Yes, we are the vanguard—but the powerful machine is already set up for roughly 99% of us.

If we should die or disappear, it won't be an accident, no matter what the carefully schemed scenario. It will be just another one of the millions of contrived murders— orchestrated by . . . you know; I don't even have to say it.

—The End (but to be continued)

Appendix A

Included in this Appendix are samples of essays sent to the media, various advocate organizations, and state and national legislators.

Privacy Is As Essential to

Life As Food, Water, and Air

What could make an award winning, educator/school CEO, with advanced degrees from the University of Virginia and Auburn University, a former Harvard Fellow, and a **Whistle Blower** concerning civil rights abuses, become a target for dangerous and deadly tricks, torture, and terrorism?

One of the most noted educators in the world in the latter 1990's, Dr. Cherubini believes he has been under 24/7 surveillance for possibly a decade, or even much longer. The probability of "spies in the backyard" became so strong at times, that he took extremely drastic measures, including staging uncharacteristic conversations and behaviors that might determine **if** there were watchers and **who** these **terrorists** were.

Then, On June 19, 2012, at 7:30 p.m., the first black Chinook helicopter (that he knows about) made several passes over his house. Highly unusual. And within one year, another five or six appeared—some hovering over the roof and grounds.

Not long after a more recent copter hovering, he noticed the huge, bright red spots on his legs and body. Was there a connection between what appeared to be radiation or microwave burns and the helicopters?

Upset, he mentioned, brashly, in the "privacy" of his home, he would sue those responsible and donate the proceeds to fight civil rights and liberty abuses. The next day, there were literal hornets' nests of police watching and tailing him in several cities and suburbs! Then, the deadly tricks began. And they continue—ever more deadly and dangerous. The stress is phenomenal. Since his hasty mention of a law suit, odd "coincidences" have been happening. One of the first was a house fire. He left his own house for fifteen minutes, and when he returned, smoke was billowing out of a neighboring house. Then, the police "presence" reached new heights—from the South to New England. Emergency vehicles suddenly proliferated. Computer breakdowns, major plumbing problems (one very dangerous), cars/trucks playing dangerous road tricks, a swooping helicopter following him down a rural highway, gas spilled beside his parked car with a cigarette butt in the middle, a dead raccoon on the front lawn, many positive readings for "bugs" in three vehicles (which miraculously stopped the day one car was taken to the police station), and much more. Some irksome, some dangerous. All uncalled for.

Again, though, the spies have been "out there" for years, Dr. Cherubini thinks, and he sees no end in sight. He cannot believe this is the America he grew up in. Just what group could command so many helicopters and emergency/law enforcement vehicles, he isn't sure, but his sources indicate that the "Patriot Act" protects those who earmark certain people (read lawful dissenters) as threats to their agenda. Further, these people can be harassed covertly or even, according to a Defense Department directive (5240 1-R, 1994) that one source mentioned, be used, without their knowledge, for remote experimentation, that is, by using high technology to remotely torment and deceive victims without leaving evidence.

Dr. Cherubini knows, too, that such tactics are **not** in

keeping with an American democracy and that any group employing such tactics—at home or abroad—should and must be questioned—and controlled! That is what our elected leaders are for—to question and control.

It Can't Happen to Me!
Or Can It?

It can't happen to me! Holocaust victims of the late 1930's and early 1940's believed this. But it **did** happen to them. Isolation. Imprisonment. Death.

Why? Sinister forces wanted the wealth of targeted groups and the power it would buy. And while the gas showers cleansed the regime of those who did not fit into the existing leadership's schema, the regime's drones extracted gold teeth from the corpses, cut the women's hair for wig making, and in some cases even excised skin from the corpses for use in furniture making. Already their jewels and gold coins, sewn into the linings of their coats and jackets, had been seized. Their homes, their art, their bank accounts found their way into the clutches of the regime's leaders. Perhaps those gassed were the lucky ones for others were used for scientific and medical experimentation. Their deaths must have been excruciating.

But **nothing** like that could ever happen again. *Or could it?*

Already, American society may be *inescapably* closer to the policed state that characterized Nazi Germany. And there will be no hiding in someone's vacant attic or basement. Today's technology can ferret out even the most secluded victim.

But it *can't* **happen to me,** you say. Don't be so sure. The wrong word or the wrong complaint. And if you've ever supported a cause not in sync with the powerful's agenda—causes like anti-war, anti-nuclear proliferation, non GMO foods, non fluoridated water, environmental issues, economic and political equity for women or minorities in the workplace, or you're against drugging hyperactive children or using the schools as recruiting stations for the armed forces, heaven forbid. You've probably gotten yourself on a **"suspicious persons"** list, which means, you bear watching.

Did you know that if you happen to be on someone's "watch" list, your "privacy"—what little you have left—suddenly evaporates. That's right. GONE!

With the technology available to them, these "watchers" can eavesdrop in your home—even your bathroom or your bedroom. They can see and hear and record **all** that goes on in your home or in your car. If you have been deemed "dangerous" enough—meaning, you are a thinking/creative person who does not accept just anything without question, then you may have been earmarked as fair game for experimentation and/or **gang stalking.** (By the way, it is common knowledge that many of the scientists and medical doctors who experimented on inmates of the Nazi concentration camps were brought to America after the war and encouraged to continue their experimentation, especially that dealing with **mind control.**)

Please, do **not** take my word for such accusations. Look up electronic assault, microwave assault, organized gang stalking, and methods of mind control on various internet sites to educate yourself. Paul Baird's site (http://www.surveillanceissues.com) provides a fairly comprehensive place to begin. Others substantiate his claims and provide additional information:

http://www.avnewstalk.com/Gang-Stalking.html
http://www.riksavisen.no/?p=501

A number of books (including Jim Keith's <u>Mass</u> <u>Control</u> and Michael F. Bell's <u>The</u> <u>Invisible</u> <u>Crime)</u> address the purpose behind such programs, programs that have been going on for over fifty years. The purpose of the experimentation is to find an expedient method of subduing and subjecting the masses in the service of the powerful. Unless **you** happen to be a member of that "club," you are *not* exempt. I know I'm not.

Recently, my husband and I visited a new art gallery and spoke with the person who was greeting visitors.

She was very much aware of the wholesale privacy invasion (not just from cell phones and computers) but in *every* aspect of our lives. "In fact," she told us, "a Jewish friend of mine, who barely managed to escape the holocaust, says that the atmosphere in today's America is increasingly like the atmosphere in Nazi Germany prior to World War II."

But that can't happen to us! you say.

What we do not realize is that **it is happening! To** *all* **of us!**

And if **we**, who are **good women** and **good men**, fail to stop this evil, *we are lost.* **LOST!**

Pets-2, Humans-2

Our house was **worse** than a toxic waste dump. The fumes that permeated every room were burning the lining of my nostrils, burning my eyes so bad that I had to keep applying wet compresses, and my throat was so sore I kept a lemon honey cough drop in my mouth to trickle relief.

I am a ***Targeted Individual***. The torture/death squads have thousands of deadly tricks, but chemical-drug releases into your house—and cars—are mainstays, along with deadly microwaves that are beamed into your home. There are many more acts of pure torture and terror that most Targeted Individuals (read **whistleblowers** and **activists**) face every day, but that is a lengthy expose on organized group, or gang, stalking.

This day I was concerned more than ever about our three dogs. They were snorting and sniffing and pawing their noses continuously, obviously gagging, as I was. I ran them outside to their large pen, and immediately got on the phone to the animal advocates, PETA and SPCA, about the poisoning of our of home and, thus, our pets.

We had already sent scores of emails and snail mails and made many dozens of phone calls to the human advocates. We visited media offices and explained the unbelievable murderous design of gang stalking. They listened, rather politely. Except for two magazine editors, media has been unresponsive to an issue that the public should be made aware of. A local human advocate group is the only one we have heard from. And we had seen and/or written and called many over the past two months after fully realizing we were Targeted Individuals.

Then, we got the call back message from PETA. Short, yes, but at least an advocacy call!

My wife and I played the message back—revealing that while most people could care less about the plight of Targeted Individuals, someone readily showed concern about our sick dogs.

That return call helped restore some of our faith in humankind. Thank you PETA, a thousand times over! If others happen to know about any advocates for humans, please let us know. There are several hundred thousand Americans, by many estimates, being systematically tortured and murdered by organized criminal group stalkers.

And how horrible are the atrocities against humans who are Targeted Individuals? One of the most representative groups for TI's is FFCHS (Freedom from Covert Harassment and Stalking), and they collect notarized statements from members: a **NO SUICIDE EVER** pact! Indeed, there are *two* good reasons for such a drastic pact. One reason goes well beyond the obvious.

America needs to know and understand more about Gang Stalking. It is MURDER. First degree. Premeditated.

Why Me?

This question surfaced within the first few days after I realized "they" were after me. Why me? At that point, I knew nothing about terms like "Organized Stalking," "Gang Stalking," "Targeted Individuals." In fact, I wouldn't even know about such things for another five months.

What I thought I knew was that various government authorities were watching us 24/7, following us, and creating havoc in our lives. Their crimes were so covert that a seventy year old couple might find "some real proof" (which attorneys like to have) impossible to produce.

In the earliest pages of my 100 Day Diary, I quickly answered the "Why Me?" question. Five months later, I was talking to a top periodical's extremely perceptive editor, and he asked, "Have you thought about answering the question, 'Why You?'"

I told him "Why Me?" was my first question. The answer was obvious: I was a *whistleblower*. In mid-September, I found out there was a "War on Whistleblowers." It was that simple. The government has a **War on Whistleblowers**; I am one, so I am unwittingly cast as "the enemy."

The editor and I talked for another fifteen or twenty minutes. He concluded by saying, again, "You really might want to answer that question—'Why Me?'—and send it to us.

We said good bye, and I felt enlightened by much of what he had said . . . except, I wondered if he had really *heard* the answer to "Why Me?"

Everything I had read said that whistleblowers were the preferred target for the government. Since we were talking fast, maybe he hadn't heard me say I was a whistleblower. (I knew he had.)

A few weeks later, I again thought I had the more complete answer to the "Why Me?" The media coverage almost two decades earlier had become phenomenal! After first seeking the spotlight on our plight (for safety concerns), there was soon more media interest than I could deal with. Regretfully, I had to turn down many features, including CNN, Phil Donohue, and People magazine. Many, many media did cover the civil rights issues that I was trying to correct in my school system, and I saw their work as a positive influence on society. Hard tracking in education is hardly fair.

Civil rights and hard tracking. Issues that did not sit well in my community. As a result, there were so many "incidents" that I thought it wise to see what the FBI could do about disruptions to normal school operations. The FBI came right over. I imagine that's when my FBI file began. So, what's wrong with that, you ask?

Quite a bit, according to researcher/writer Marshall Thomas, who did a Targeted Individuals assessment. He found that targets were chosen from a database of many millions, and a cumulative weighted score was given to each name.

Whistleblowers were found to be targeted at a highly disproportionate figure for their number in society. Other key criteria categorized by Thomas included civil rights activity, as well as having an FBI file!

I automatically began doing the math in my head.

Number one by all counts, I was a whistleblower on civil rights issues, and I had called in the FBI. Three out of three top reasons!

Twenty years ago, I thought most anyone would see these three top reasons as, if not laudable, at least merit worthy. Certainly not as reasons to be governmentally targeted for harassment, torture, and murder! Today, there is probably not one targeted individual who is not in disbelief that a government can choose targets for such arbitrary reasons and continue to get away with it decade after decade. Sadly, MK ULTRA and COINTELPRO (CIA and FBI programs) continued, but continued as if on steroids—exponentially more deadly with forty to sixty years of chemical and electronic weaponry advances. With the advent of the "Patriot Act," the military and the quasi military are more than ready to finish trampling what is left of freedom, liberty, and democracy.

You and I have heard this same spiel so many times before. But the looming question is—*what can we do about it?*

One thing we can do is talk. During the past (misguided?) fifteen years, I *have* talked. Yes, I talked at peace conferences and peace rallies. I marched and waved signs for peace. I recorded my own peace CD and put one of the songs on "My Space." The next day my computer was dead, along with all of the musical information that we had not properly backed up! I also talked on the phone everyday to relatives, and I would hear myself saying in the course of the discourse, things like: the CIA is guilty of assassinations just as it is complicit in heroin trafficking or prostitution rings. Or, it's a travesty that Homeland Security can get all the money it wants while necessary programs are being abandoned.

If talking, marching, and recording protest tunes can be thought of as *activism*, note that dissenters/activists are among the highly preferred government targets.

I am doing the math again, and it's beginning to seem as if I'm hell bent on being targeted for torture and murder! The truth is, however, I did not realize until eight months ago that the government even involved itself in organized "gang" stalking or "no touch slow kill" programs. (Microwaves and chemicals = "slow kill.")

Above, six mammoth reasons **WHY**. But, will "they" have other reasons? Because "they" are covert/clandestine, I can't even say with 100% certainty who "they" are. I can with great certainty determine that "they" have extreme power and unlimited resources!

From my extensive (but not exhaustive) research, it can easily be noted that "they" avoid the reasons for targeting that are most profound, such as the subject is a whistleblower or an activist. Instead, "they" usually conjure up reasons such as the person is a prostitute, a pervert, a pedophile (they should know a lot about the hot button sex issues!), a drug user, a racist, or a terrorist. (I consider myself, like most of the targets, 180° opposite on all counts.) Yet, all the perpetrators need is a word or a jocular comment that one might utter during the thousands of hours of 24/7 surveillance That word or comment is taken out of context and used to vilify, then destroy, the victim. And should "they" not get that word, "they" can *induce* whatever "they" need through chemicals, drugs, and/or microwaves (old technology fine tuned to be used in the most horrifying ways possible). Recall MK ULTRA of the 60's and 70's; Dr. Robert Duncan, former CIA, says the program never stopped!   Dr. Rauni Kilde tells us that brain microwaving can induce practically *anything*!

I have absorbed a lot of information in the past two decades, both from mainstream and alternative news, and had heard only a brief reference to organized, group, or gang stalking. At the time, I even wondered about the validity of the story. But when the topic surfaced as I was researching government mind control, I realized that the world of true horror I was reading about and seeing on film was the same phenomenon that was occurring in my own life. The same government organized stalking was happening to *ME*! All the many symptoms of microwave assault. The ravages of chemical assault in home and cars. The catastrophic direct energy assault. The near accidents caused by perpetrators on the roads. The extensive damage to property. The character smear, the isolation, the 24/7 surveillance of home and cars. The hoards of criminal perpetrators ready to do most anything for a tank of gas or a few drugs.

Government organized stalking makes COINTELPRO look like a Sunday school picnic, according to the late Ted Gunderson, who was a district FBI chief for several decades.

Not one single American deserves such a clandestine torture, murder program.

Who is responsible for this torture/murder program?

Most sources I have found implicate the government. More specifically, the military and the CIA. I think more government entities are involved—many that must be subservient to the large power wielders.

Accounts by other targeted individuals tell how astounded they are when friends and family desert them instantly upon hearing the lies—distortions of truth—that perpetrators tell about actions that TI's have "supposedly" taken. I find such "desertion" appalling and reprehensible, especially considering the horrendous atrocities the government agency "handling" the perpetrators could be involved in itself.

A quick, partial glance at the index of <u>Static</u>, by Amy and David Goodman, shows topics under CIA including: heroin market, kidnapping by; propaganda contracts of; smear campaigns by; and torture promoted by. There are many more entries, but these rank among the worst. Another author, James W. Douglass, in <u>JFK and the Unspeakable</u>, lists in his index for the CIA: undermining peace initiatives; assassination program; assassination plots against Castro, Lumumba, and Sukarno; and assassination of JFK.

Although the lists in the previous paragraph may be more than damning, many of us feel we are seeing only the tip of the iceberg. The CIA is covert. They answer to NO one about their clandestine dirty work, and their funding is virtually unlimited. Their projects include LSD and electronic mind control. The latter, started in the 1990's, is now perfected. Ask any targeted individual.

I think, often several times a day, of the American political family I admire and love most. Each day I must wonder about how many of them were targeted by our own government agencies: two, three, possibly four? Even to allow one to be targeted and murdered and to do *nothing* about it is too much to bear.

The agency that President Gerald Ford and James W. Douglass saw as guilty of assassination has not only escaped even a slap on the hand, it has become the most powerful entity in the world, along with their parent, the military! We Americans and our elected leaders have allowed it to happen.

Do "they" know that I so admire the political family "they" are so intent upon murdering and degrading? Of course! With their 24/7 surveillance, "they" know *everything*, and they employ the worst kind of covert tactics imaginable to learn everything a person does, says, or thinks!

But their tactics don't stop at surveillance. Surveillance, 24/7 is only the starting point. They are obsessed with directed energy weapons—furtive killing tools which can induce heart attacks and diseases such as cancer or leukemia and with microwave mind control technology.

I, too, thought, "Me? Get mind controlled? Impossible!" Even as I was thinking those thoughts, I was being mind controlled. Old technology, perfected. So are the chemicals and drugs. Twenty to sixty years of LSD manipulation. No telling what potentially lethal variations of LSD and other chemicals and bio-toxins have been perfected during that time.

Chemicals and microwaves. We are getting both.

When will the assaults stop!? Whistleblower, Dr. Robert Duncan intimates that *it's too late*. I tend to agree with the expert, Duncan. Unless—that *media snowball* rolls fast in the right direction.

Who will be the next CHE? The catalyst? No one! NO *ONE*! It will take *all of us* to dissolve the monstrous covert military evil *we* have all allowed to take over. The *"Silent Holocaust,"* as gang stalking is often called, is the *worst criminal atrocity the world has ever known*. It will grow and devour us unless action is taken! *NOW!*

Appendix B

The following pages contain a few samples of the hundreds of letters sent to the media, legislators and human advocacy groups.

March 23, 2014

Senator _____
Dirksen Senate Office Building
Washington, D.C. 20510

Dear Senator _____:

My husband and I went by your Burlington, VT, office in February to relate information about a phenomenon that seems to be pervading the country. As landowners in Vermont, we felt that you, because of your record on protecting the civil liberties of Americans, would be a good person to investigate the issue.

This phenomenon targets certain law abiding individuals (read whistleblowers, single women, dissenters, and activists, or those who question the authority of those in power). The targeted individuals, or TI's, are put under surveillance for a number of years and are subject to organized stalking (sponsored by government, our research tells us, probably through black operations). Among other tactics, the perpetrators use electronic harassment with supposedly non lethal weapons, which, because of their effects on the human body, end up being quite lethal, to torture the TI's. The purpose, research tells us, is experimentation in mind control.

Sounds like science fiction, doesn't it? But it is not. Too much information exists (both on the internet and in print) about the technology, the government patents, Department of Defense directives, the "Patriot Act," and what people who say they have suffered from this phenomenon have written about it. Because of the weaponry used and the organized method of isolating subjects, what is occurring remains largely unprovable, thus deniable.

I know you have a busy schedule; however, we Americans depend on those of you in our legislative branch to safeguard our safety, our privacy, and our right to call into question issues and practices not in the best interest of our citizenry. Please have your staff research this phenomenon thoroughly and inform other lawmakers to do likewise. Such tactics and weaponry should be outlawed in America.

Please keep me informed about what you discover. I will be happy to assist in any way possible.

Sincerely,

March 12, 2014

Senator _____
United States Senate
Hart Senate Office Building
Washington, D.C. 20510

Dear Senator _____:

My husband and I wish to express our gratitude to you and your staff for exposing the CIA's reprehensible behavior in illegally spying on the very people who are to have oversight on its activities.

Unless groups such as these receive more than a hand slap for activities not in the best interest of the citizens they are supposed to serve, our democracy will cease to exist and the majority of us will find ourselves slaves to the powerful.

I have included several articles which address government sponsored programs that probably need a great deal *more* oversight than they are currently receiving. Perhaps your committee can investigate these issues and bring them to the public's attention.

Please continue your good work. You and people like you who have the integrity to question a corrupt system are the *only hope* for our country. Please let us know if there is anything we can do to help.

Sincerely,

Representative _____
Rayburn House Office Building
Washington, D.C. 20515

Dear Representative _____:

I read with interest your initiative in seeking the abolishment of the Pentagon's 1033 program which militarizes local law enforcement agencies. We live near Murfreesboro, TN, which I understand is one of the small towns where such things are currently taking place. Good work. You are on the right track for insuring that democracy remains democracy.

I would also like to ask you and your staff to investigate another matter that involves violation of the civil liberties of law abiding Americans. This involves targeting individuals for long term surveillance, character smearing, and electronic assault by microwaves and microchips. These individuals, or TI's, are targeted because they are whistleblowers, activists for civil rights, the environment, peace—anything that does not fit the agenda of the power brokers. My husband fits into this category; as school superintendent in a Southwest Georgia school system in the mid 1990's, he took measures to correct civil rights abuses in the system, much to the disgruntlement of the local power structure.

Though the scenario I paint seems like science fiction, it is not. The technology exists and has since the 1950's. The enclosed article provides a starting place for research. Please inform me about what you discover and what can be done about it. I will be glad to help.

Sincerely,

May 10, 2014

Senator _____
Washington, D.C. 20510

Dear Senator _____ :

John F. Kennedy Profile in Courage award winner, Dr. Corkin Cherubini, *fears* for his life and that of his family. He and his wife have been assaulted with directed energy weapons, and since mid February, his house, yard, and vehicles have been saturated with what he suspects are "Slow Kill" (read lethal) chemicals.

NOBODY, including CDC, EPA, and their Tennessee affiliates seem to be able to offer any viable help in discovering the source of this chemical dousing. It seems to be remotely controlled to assault him at random moments, but especially when he is researching "what could be going on?" on the internet or when he *mentions* action he should take to put an end to COVERT *murder* of two seventy year old retired educators who spent their working lives attempting to make a DIFFERENCE in the lives and attitudes of young people—many of whom were "at risk" youngsters.

The media and most advocacy groups seem uninterested in pursuing this issue, which has been posed to them as a issue affecting citizens throughout America.

We have heard from one U. S. Representative's local office and Senate and House of Representative's offices in Tennessee's legislature as well as from animal adovcates, PETA and SPCA, who offered to help us shield our dogs from the chemicalized atmosphere in our home.

U.S. Senate and House of Representative members in New Hampshire, Vermont, and Maine, where we also own property, have been informed. NO RESPONSE!

The Senate Oversight Committee for Intelligence matters has been informed. NO RESPONSE!

WHAT IS GOING ON??? Are you guys and gals in Washington willing to allow constituents in our country to be **MURDERED** while you twiddle your thumbs and say ho-hum?

I certainly hope not! It's time for those of you in power (if indeed you really have any power) to do something **positive** for America and its citizens.

Sincerely,

April 25, 2014

Newstips at Globe
The Boston Globe
135 Morrissey Blvd.
Boston, MA 02125

I would like to make your staff aware of an issue which threatens the very existence of any privacy, even privacy of thought, we, as Americans, expect. This issue is known as **Organized Gang Stalking**. It is characterized by 24/7 surveillance, even in one's own home or vehicles, harassment, character smears, isolation from family and friends, assault with directed energy weaponry and/or drugs and chemicals, induced thoughts or dreams or aggressive actions (which may include suicide), and may end with the victim's murder, either through induced heart attack or as a result of continuous directed energy assaults which cause leukemia, cancer, and other lethal maladies. Victims are generally innocent American citizens who most often are whistleblowers, activists, women, especially single ones, minorities, or those who fail to rubberstamp the local, state, or national government agendas.

Oddly, few people—and we have spoken to many—are even aware that such a program exists, even though estimates of the number of victims range between three to four hundred thousand to over a million. There seems to be a media blackout on the topic. However, there are books written about the topic and numerous internet and You Tube sites that provide information.

We are hoping that someone on your staff will investigate this dreadful phenomenon and expose it.

Only with knowledge can victims even begin to deal with what may be happening to them. Only when society becomes aware that we may well be headed for an existence in which we are puppets to be controlled to sate the whims of the powerful, will we be able (hopefully) to put a stop to Organized Gang Stalking and its attendant atrocities.

PLEASE HELP! I will be most happy to supply additional information, including book titles and internet sites, not mentioned in the enclosed articles.

Sincerely,

March 30, 2014

Weekly Edition Editor
Christian Science Monitor
210 Massachusetts Avenue
Boston, MA 02115-3195

I am writing to you because your magazine has always been on the cutting edge in informing Americans about issues that affect their spiritual, social, and political well-being. Today, there seems to be an evil lurking just beneath the surface of their daily existence, but hardly anyone is aware of it so that appropriate action can be taken to eliminate it.. The enclosed article refers to **"the silent holocaust"** which is taking place, not just in this country but worldwide, at this very moment. Whistleblowers, activists, and women, especially single women, and the elderly seem to be considered easy targets.

If the perpetrators of this "silent holocaust" are allowed to proceed unchecked, our spiritual selves must be denied because the perpetrators will condone faith no more than they will condone creativity or individual thought or problem solving.

Please investigate these issues and help to inform your readership as you see fit. Please keep me informed about what your magazine can do to bring this issue to the attention of the public. I will be glad to help in any way possible.

Sincerely,

March 14, 2014

Managing Editor
First Things
35 East 21st Street
6th Floor
New York, NY 10010

I recently read the article, "On Creative Minorities" in the January, 2014, issue of your magazine. What struck me as apropos about the article was Jonathan Sacks's assessment that the prophet Jeremiah was telling the Israelites to use their **creativity** as a means for succeeding in keeping their religious and cultural heritage intact in a hostile environment.

The articles that accompany this note imply that evil forces in our world intend to quelch, not only an individual's creativity, but his or her individuality as well—through fear and mind control. Unfortunately, few people seem aware of the technology that allows evil forces to progress unimpeded.

Perhaps you and your staff could investigate these issues and get the word out before what is being called *"the silent holocaust"* progresses irrevocably.

Sincerely,

March 14, 2014

Editor
Prism Renew
P. O. Box 367
Wayne, PA 19087

Dear Editor:

Christian women, as well as the men in their lives, need to become informed about the evil lurking just beneath the surface of their daily existence so they can take the appropriate action. The enclosed article refers to **"the silent holocaust"** which is taking place, not just in this country but worldwide, at this very moment. Women, especially single women, seem to be considered easy targets.

If the perpetrators of this "silent holocaust" are allowed to proceed unchecked, our spiritual selves, that part of us that is holy, must be denied because the perpetrators will condone faith no more than they will condone creativity or individual thought or problem solving.

Please investigate these issues and help to inform your readership as you see fit.

Sincerely,

AARP CEO
601 East St., N.E.
Washington, D.C. 20049

My husband and I have visited your Burlington, VT, office, sent letters to as well as called your Washington office, and plan to visit the Nashville office in the next few days. Though individuals we spoke with listened politely to our concerns, we have had *no* response from them.

The subject in question should concern *all* citizens, but seniors, especially those who have been activists or whistleblowers or who have diligently prepared themselves financially for their "golden years" may find themselves targeted for what is called ***organized gang stalking***. Research says there is often no rhyme nor reason as to who gets targeted, but those with lucrative estates are often fair game for the stalkers. The last thing seniors need to worry about when they should be enjoying retirement and their grandchildren is a group of criminals out to ruin them.

The enclosed essays provide more information about this phenomenon. ***Please*** have someone on your staff research the topics discussed and decide how best to inform your members. Ignorance may be bliss—until the moment one faces either death at the hands of the perpetrators or destruction of one's life, one's family, and one's reputation. If my husband or I can be of assistance in this task, please let us know. Also, please keep us informed about what you discover.

Sincerely,

May 3, 2014

Dr. _____

FIRE

170 South Independence Mall, West

Suite 510

Philadelphia, PA 19106

Dear Sir:

I understand that you are an adjunct scholar with the Cato Institute as well as the co-founder of FIRE. Since these foundations study issues in society and help to create policy for the United States government, I am writing to you to alert you to a frightening phenomenon that seems to be pervading American society: what some writers are calling *"The Silent Holocaust."*

I am sending an essay that describes my husband's situation as a *Targeted Individual* who has been the victim of what is called *Organized Gang Stalking* for at least a decade, perhaps more. This phenomenon primarily targets whistleblowers, activists, dissidents, writers, women, especially single ones, and minority groups, although *anyone* seems to be fair game for the perpetrators. The stalking involves 24/7 surveillance, harassment, character smears, isolation from family and friends, electronic assault with microwaves, masers, drugs and chemicals, and induced dreams and thoughts. The end result is generally death, either by induced heart attack or stroke, suicide, or from a disease caused by repeated ELF waves. The purpose? Research tells us experimentation in mind control with the ultimate purpose of mass control.

There seems to be a media blackout on this topic, and as

a result, almost no one we talk to—and believe me, we've talked to scores of people—has ever heard of this phenomenon. *The public needs to be informed.* Public policy on this matter needs to be framed and legislation put in place to end this crime and dissolve any organization responsible for it.

PLEASE HELP! I will be willing to do what I can to help you. I would appreciate your keeping me informed about your progress.

Sincerely,

To: Sierra Club and
      Sierra Club Electees

The enclosed articles make reference to a phenomenon that seems to be pervading the lives of those of us who care about America and democracy, who stand up for what is right for the majority of our citizens, and who dare to question and remedy practices that are not in the best interest of that majority.

Please inform yourself about the phenomenon of gang stalking (or organized stalking) and electronic harassment and abuse. Once you are informed, it is easier to protect yourself. Also, examine ways that we, the people, can demand that these abuses be outlawed and punished.

Sincerely,

Electronic Frontier Foundation
815 Eddy Street
San Francisco, CA 94109

Thank you for the work you are doing to put a stop to the wholesale collection of our telephone and computer data and emails by groups associated with the federal government. The unwarranted surveillance of innocent American citizens is against all principles of our democracy.

I have enclosed a couple of essays that address this problem as well as unwarranted surveillance using electronic equipment to track individuals and to spy on them with pin hole type cameras and microphones, both in their homes and in their vehicles. I'm not sure whether this technology is addressed by your foundation or not, but I hope it is.

Sincerely,

March 19, 2014

National Organization for Women
150 West 28th Street
New York, New York 10001

I spoke with someone in your office earlier today about this matter and said I would be sending more explanatory information.

The enclosed article refers to what has been called "the silent holocaust" by a number of writers. The implications of this scenario are bleak for humanity, but especially for women—thinking women, creative women, single women—who even in today's society are too often seen as less capable or deserving than their male counterparts. Mainstream, male dominated media does not seem interested in investigating issues discussed in the article. In fact, hardly anyone I talk to is even aware that they exist. But they do exist. Too much information exists on the technology and its illegal, inhumane use—past and present. If the men of this world won't take responsibility for averting disaster, I suppose we women will have to do it.

I am hoping that you and your staff will take the time to research the issues mentioned in the article. I know that much of it sounds like science fiction. But even science fiction has a way of finding its way into reality. Please tell me what I can do to help. I would really like to have feedback on your thoughts.

Sincerely,

April 27, 2014

Editor
USA Today
7950 Jones Branch Drive
McLean, VA 22108

On Friday I spoke to a very perceptive individual at the Customer Service desk for USA Today and told him my story. Not only did he listen attentively, he suggested that I contact you with the story and my concerns.

On Saturday, I attempted to email you. However, my email was interrupted before I had finished it, and I think only a part of it was sent to you. As a result, I am sending an essay that describes my situation as a *Targeted Individual* who has been the victim of what is called *Organized Gang Stalking* for at least a decade, perhaps more. This phenomenon primarily targets **whistleblowers, activists, dissidents, writers, women**, especially single ones, and **minority groups**, although *anyone* seems to be fair game for the perpetrators. The stalking involves 24/7 surveillance, harassment, character smears, isolation from family and friends, electronic assault with microwaves, masers, drugs, and chemicals, and induced dreams and thoughts. The end result is generally death, either by induced heart attack or stroke, suicide, or from a disease caused by repeated ELF waves. The purpose? Research tells us experimentation in **mind control** with the ultimate purpose of **mass control.**

There seems to be a media blackout on this topic, and as A result, almost no one we talk to—and believe me, we've talked to scores of people—has ever heard of this phenomenon. *The public needs to be informed.* Legislation needs to be put in place to end this crime and dissolve any organization responsible for it. I can see a triple Pulitzer awaiting the investigative reporter(s) who are tenacious and brave enough to seek the truth about this crime and help to put an end to it. PLEASE HELP!

Sincerely,

P.S. Since all our communications seem to become compromised, I will send several copies of this letter to you.

Appendix C

The War on Whistleblowers

(Reprinted with permission from www.stopcovertwar.com site.)

As corruption continues to grow in all sectors of our society, we can only blame ourselves for our continued reluctance to pass laws that adequately protect those brave souls who have put their lives and careers on the line to stand against greed, corruption, and outright disregard for the health and safety of the American public.

Whistleblowing results in disaster for those reporting corruption. The whistleblower is tried and convicted, and sentenced to life in prison. The victims will never be told what the charges are, will never be allowed to examine the evidence against them, nor will he/she be allowed to confront their accusers. A secret campaign of stalking and harassment constructs for the victim a prison without walls. Exposing corruption is now a crime in our country and never goes unpunished.

Those honest folks who try to right a wrong often lose their jobs and are blacklisted for the remainder of their lives. Much of the time the victims are stalked and harassed in ways which cause them to appear paranoid. Their marriages often end in divorce due to the constant strain of being targeted. Friends and family members cannot understand why the victim will not "get help," and imply that the victim needs psychiatric care. Any business venture attempted will be sabotaged into bankruptcy. Finances are thus eroded to such an extent that the victim may become homeless.

The perpetrators of these crimes continue to follow

the victim everywhere, spreading lies about him/her, so that the victim's character is so badly assassinated that he or she cannot build a new life. New acquaintances are scared away or induced to participate in the campaign against the victim. The victim may accidentally find employment for a period of time but is often harassed out of the job after only a few weeks. Bosses and co-workers are secretly brought "on line" to participate in the harassment and sabotage of work until the victim quits or is fired. This is how an intelligent, hard working, honest human being is pushed into the street and becomes homeless.

How long will we continue to punish the innocent while the guilty remain free to spread crime and corruption throughout the country? How many scandals will there have to be before Congress will pass laws effective enough to put a stop to this most heinous of crimes? Why is there no outrage . . . ? Why do we do nothing while war is being waged against the most innocent and honest members of our society? What message does this send to our children? Don't report corruption or you will pay for it with your life. Be a "team player" and keep your mouth shut. Honesty doesn't count. Just let the crooks do business as usual. What a sorry state of affairs!

Bibliography

The books and articles I relied on for my research came mostly from my personal library—especially until mid-February when I began to use the internet again. (For months I felt it was imprudent to even try to look up information on the internet about what I suspected was going on. Ditto for checking out library books.) Several weeks after the hundred day diary entries had been completed, I found a book in my library that I wish I had discovered sooner and used as a reference. The title is Static, 2006, and the authors you certainly know of from Democracy Now—Amy Goodman and David Goodman. I looked at the index. Under CIA, the following entries appeared:

- disinformation disseminated by, 95-96

- and heroin market, 97

- kidnappings by, 21, 24-25, 29-32, 37-39

- propaganda contracts of, 70

- smear campaigns by, 96-97

- torture promoted by, 149, 151-153, 160-164,   250, 251

There are many other entries under this topic, but I find it indicative of the worst when most of my references include similar index topics.

My initial research source was Paul Baird's "The Truth About Secret Weapons and the Involuntary Testing of Those Weapons on Civilians" (found at http://www.surveillanceissues.com/). Several quotes from this site are illustrative of a world of which most people have little or no knowledge.

"Most people fear corrupt media representatives and covert agency people (e.g., the CIA) more than anyone else, and with good reason, so much so that mere mention of their involvement [with TI's] instills such fear that it's an absolute conversation stopper; evidence of the worst terrorism imaginable."

In another Paul Baird paragraph:

" . . . corruptible court and law enforcement officials, psychiatrists, and others help to discredit those presenting the truth. . . . Many agency targets, as well as agency whistlblowers have been destroyed this way. Honest psychiatrists who try to blow the whistle . . . are . . . murdered."

I thank God I have this Paul Baird article:

"Persons of interest (both good and bad) are monitored via satellite 24/7; many are also tormented and tortured through the use of satellite-based directed energy weapons and psychotropic attacks using neurophones (voice to skull technology), mind reading technologies, and so on . . . . Banned/censored writers, whistleblowers, and anti-crime campaigners, etc., also have harassment 24/7 . . . ."

A source with much information is www.peacepink.ning.com

Another source is that of long time TI Robert Wood's internet site, "Targeted Individuals," 2011. Wood emphasizes:

"There are covert crimes being committed against innocent and virtually defenseless American citizens and citizens of other countries, as well. I am one of these persons."

"Virtually defenseless" is how my wife and I feel much of the time since no one, not law enforcement, not the legal community, not advocacy groups, not our legislators seem to be able to offer much in the way of assistance, even when they wish to do so.

The web site bibliotecapleyades also offers a wealth of information on mind control as does www.torturedinamerica.

Other sources include:

Albrecht, Katherine, and McIntyre, Liz. Spychips: How Major Corporations and Government Plan to Track Your Every Move With RFID. Nashville, TN: Nelson Current, 2005.

Alexander, Michelle. The New Jim Crow: Mass Incarceration in the Age of Colorblindness. New York: The New Press, 2012.

Babacek, Moimir. "Psychotronic and Electromagnetic Weapons: Remote Control of the Human Nervous System." March 3, 2014. @ www.globalsearch.ca/psychotronic-and-electromagnetic-weapons-Remote-control-of

Barker, Allen L. "Essays on Mind Control, Part III, Mental Firewalls." February 17, 2002. www.jbhfile.com/PartIII-mental-firewalls

Begich, Dr. Nick. "Bio-Hazards of Extremely Low Frequencies (ELF)." www.earthpulse.com/.../subcategory.asp? . . .

Begich, Dr. Nick. Controlling the Human Mind: The Technologies of Political Control or Tools for Peak Performance. Anchorage, Alaska: Earthpulse Press, Inc., 2006.

Bell, Michael F. The Invisible Crime: Illegal Microchip Implants and Their Use Against Humanity. Chandler, AZ: Brighton Publishing, 2011.

Douglass, James W. JFK and the Unspeakable. New York: Simon and Schuster, 2008.

Duncan, Dr. Robert. How to Tame a Demon: A Short Practical Guide to Organized Intimidation, Stalking, Electronic Torture, and Mind Control. Boise, Idaho: Higher Order Thinkers Publishing, 2014.

Duncan, Dr. Robert. The Matrix Deciphered: Psychic Warfare, 2006. From Thoughtlessness23 website.

Ferber, Markus. "Gang Stalking Is Murder." @www.gangstalkingismurder.wordpress.com

Gunderson, Ted. "The Conspiracy of Silence: The Documentary They Don't Want You to See." http://educateyourself.org/tg/tgvideosandbooks1sep02.s

Gillum, Jack. "Police Keep Quiet About Cell-Tracking Technology," The Associated Press, March 22, 2014.

Greenwald, Robert, "War on Whistleblowers: Free Press and the National Security State." Documentary (66 minutes). Brave New Foundation, 2013.

Hall, Dr. John. A New Breed: Satellite Terrorism in America. New York: Strategic Book Publishing, 2009.

Jaspin, Elliot. Buried in Bitter Waters: The Hidden History of Racial Cleansing in America. New York: Basic Books, 2008.

Jansen, Derrick. "Tricks of the Trade: Alfred McCoy on How the CIA Got Involved in Global Drug Trafficking," The Sun, May, 2003.

Keith, Jim. Mass Control: Engineering Human Consciousness. Lilburn, GA: IllumiNet Press, 1999.

Kilde, Dr. Rauni Leena, M.D. "Microwave Mind Control: Modern Torture And Control Mechanisms Eliminating Human Rights and Privacy." March 17, 2008. At www://riksavisen.no/?p=501

Kilde, Dr. Rauni Leena, M.D. "Microchip Implants, Mind Control, and Cybernetics." www.educate-yourself.org/. . .implantsmcandcy. . .

Kirkland, Nicholas. "Law Enforcement Complicity in Electronic Stalking and Mind Control Activities." @http://educateyourself.org/cn/electronicstalkingand lawenforcementcomplicity07augo8

Kirkland, Nicholas. "Nicholas Kirkland's Neurological Warfare and United States Experiments." @ http://targetedindividualscanada.wordpress.com/2011/0 4/08

Krayan, Jewel. Electronic Torture, Electronic Rape: Technology and Gang Stalking at the Post Office. West Conshokoken, PA: Infinity Publications, 2012.

Lawson, David Authur. Terrorist Stalking in America. Miami, Florida: Scrambling News, 2001. Excerpts available in "Organized Stalking by Groups" @ www.multistalkervictims.org/catchcanada/organized stalking.htm

Lendman, Steve. "Electromagnetic Frequency Mind Control Weapons," January, 2011. www. sjlendman.blogspot.com/elecromanget. . .

Mars, Jim. The Terror Conspiracy. New York: The Disinformation Co., 2006.

Mathias, Barbara, and French, Mary Ann. Forty Ways to Raise a Non-Racist Child. New York: Harper Collins, 1996.

Mayer, Jane. The Dark Side. New York: Anchor Books, 2009.

McCoy, Alfred. Politics of Heroin: CIA Complicity in the Global Drug Trade. New York: Harper Collins, 2003.

"Microwave Weapons." @ http://electronicharassment.weebly.com/microwave-weapons.html

Pittman M., Rene. Remote Brain Targeting, Revised Edition, 2012.

Poet, Sharon Rose. www.targetedinamerica.com

Shielding, Dr. Duncan. "Freedom From Covert Harassment and Surveillance." @www.freedomfchs.com/shielding/dr-duncan-shielding

Smith, Norris, and Messina, Lynn, eds. Homeland Security. New York: H. Wilson Co., 2004.

Sullivan, Elizabeth. My Life Changed Forever. West Conshohoken, PA: Infinity Publications, 2008.

Thorn, Victor. "The White House War Against Whistleblowers," May 16, 2013 @ www.americanfreepress.net

Vollmann, William. "Uncovering My FBI File," Harper's Magazine, September, 2013, 39-47.

"Western Spy Agencies Build 'Cyber Magicians' to Manipulate Online Discourse," February 25, 2014. @ http://rt.com/news/five-eyes-online-manipulation-deception-564/

Williams, Max. The Silent Massacre, Ebook@ starseedresistence.com/media/The%20SILENT%20MASSACRE.pdf

Wood, Robert. "Targeted Individuals" @
www.truedemocracy.net

You Tube Videos:
"Coast to Coast" interview with Michael F. Bell
and Roger Tolces, Feb. 14, 2013.
"Coast to Coast" program. "Massive NSA
Surveillance," Jan. 29, 2014.
"Coast to Coast" program. "Technologies Used to
Manipulate People," July 28, 2012.
"Gang Stalking: America's Cointelpro Democracy."
"Gang Stalking-Counterintelligence: Former Agent
Reveals New FBI."
"Organized Gang Stalking."
"Organized Gang Stalking and Electronic
Harassment."
Roger Tolces. "U.S. Government Torture and
Electronic Harassment."
Roger Tolces. "The Surveillance Police State and
Electronic Harassment."
"The End Game: Steve Quayle on Gang Stalking."

Afterword

Additions, Deletions, Corrections, Rethinking

I glanced back over the unproofed contents and wondered why I had said a few things. Possibly because I was thinking in a more "stream-of-consciousness" mode.

One such thing was my saying that I might follow orders from "above" even if I were not sure they were ethical. The connotation of the passage shocked me. If I thought that what I was directed to do was wrong or if it would unnecessarily hurt someone, I could not do it. If I had a family to feed, I would look for another job. Of course, there are times we don't fully realize that a particular directive may be questionable. When the boss directs us to do something, we often respond without question. Yet, if we suspect or if we know the directive will result in serious consequences (such as the surveillance, harassment, torture, and murder typical of Gang Stalking), wouldn't we want to look into the issue thoroughly?

Generally, we did not expect a response or follow-up from letters to the media or political offices. We did, however, get some response. A welcome surprise.

Though Vermont senators did not respond in writing, we did have a pleasant visit at their offices. One of the items we emphasized was the negative effects of our surveillance state. Several months later, we were astounded that one of these individuals was introducing measures to curtail at least some of the surveillance horrors. A welcome first step, even though additional measures need to be put in place to end the surveillance of Targeted Individuals who are law abiding American citizens. (Why? Because Gang Stalking could not exist without surveillance of our homes, cars, and environs.)

"Gang Stalking." Not a good term for the program it represents, but at least it expresses some of the negativity. It is misleading, however, since most people conclude, "Oh, yeah. We've heard about these street gangs." Writer, Vic Livingston, on an Alex Jones site, sees the terms generally used to describe what is essentially a murder program as euphemistic or as misnomers. I immediately clarify what Gang Stalking really is to most listeners: it's a *government stalking torture murder program*. Their reactions vary wildly.

I just think we need to term it as it is, not shroud evil in an euphemistic cloak.